CHUSITA
FASHION FEVER

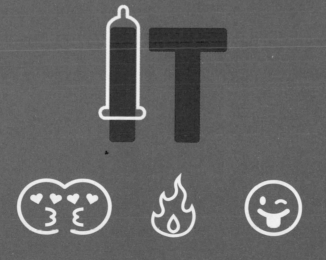

READY FOR IT

[Imprint]
MAKE YOUR MARK
NEW YORK

[Imprint]
MAKE YOUR MARK

A part of Macmillan Publishing Group, LLC
175 Fifth Avenue, New York, NY 10010

Library of Congress Control Number: 2018936701

ISBN 978-1-250-13388-5 (hardcover)

Our books may be purchased in bulk for promotional, educational, or business use. Please contact your local bookseller or the Macmillan Corporate and Premium Sales Department at (800) 221-7945 ext. 5442 or by e-mail at MacmillanSpecialMarkets@macmillan.com.

Illustrations by Maria Llovet
Imprint logo designed by Amanda Spielman
Originally published in Spain by RBA in 2016

First U.S. edition, 2018

1 3 5 7 9 10 8 6 4 2

Thieves of this book are not wired
to find a love strong and true,
for honesty is the first thing required
for turning one into two.

fiercereads.com

IF I WERE YOU, I'D KEEP HOLD OF ME 👍

CONTENTS

LET'S . . .

INTRODUCTION

LET'S TALK ABOUT SEX
BY CHUSITA

Right, can somebody please explain this to me: Why don't people talk more openly about sex? About sex, yes, SEX, SEX, SEX . . . that thing! We've had enough of avoiding calling things by their proper names, skirting around the issue, feeling ashamed, and only talking about sex in hushed voices. It's the 21st century, for goodness' sake! The time has come to stop beating around the bush . . . and you know it!

Has desire begun to awaken in your body? Are you just starting to experience sexuality and aren't quite sure what it's all about yet? You've just got going but you want to learn more? Well, this is **THE BOOK FOR YOU**! I can provide you with extensive answers, ideas, and food for thought, while making you laugh at the same time! All of this is accompanied by suggestive drawings and comics that will leave you with your mouth wide-open. Are you in? If I were you . . . **I'D TRUST ME**!

You might be wondering why I decided to write a book like this. The answer is simple: after reading the comments on my videos and all the messages viewers have sent me, I've found that you're all **PRETTY LOST** when it comes to sex. I started my YouTube channel a while back, not knowing that what you really needed was . . . personal advice! So one of my sections became "From Me to You," where I

addressed these worries. Worry upon worry about relationships, feelings, and sexual encounters. And I've realized that everyone needs even more ways of finding this information.

To be honest, **I'M NOT SURPRISED**. With so many taboos surrounding it, sex lies somewhere between the mythical and the unknown. It was the same for me: when I first encountered sex, I had never spoken about it with my parents, and in my school, which was Catholic, I hadn't been taught much more than the basic concepts of sexual reproduction.

With the small amount I had learned from talking to my friends and what I could glean from the teen magazines of my time, I started to get some idea of what it was all about. Although, when **THE MOMENT CAME**, I realized that I hardly knew anything at all.

© Errebeene

P.S. As a vlogger, I've gained so much from my followers and their comments, and I couldn't have written this book without them.

Thank you for believing in me!

 CHUSITA
FASHION
FEVER

Warning!
If you've ever sent me a question, it could be featured in this book. I hope you find the answer useful! But don't worry, because I won't expose you. No real names are mentioned in here.

Confidential

Thinking about it now, I realize just how lost I really was. And I know that, if I'd known then what I know now, I would have enjoyed my sexuality so much more, right from the start. That's why I decided to write a book like this. **I'M NOT A SEXOLOGIST**, not even close, but I've gone through the same kinds of things that most teenagers do, and now that I'm a little older, I know what it's all about. It seems as though we really need a book for young people that explains sexuality, from the first experiences to the act itself, without any censorship. If I'd had this book when I was younger, it would've helped me a lot!

I went through **A NUMBER OF PHASES**, which made me feel very insecure. I felt uncomfortable getting naked; I didn't really know if what I was feeling was normal or not; if the changes to my body were supposed to happen; if what I was doing was okay. Was I going too fast, or not fast enough? Now, after a few steady relationships and with adolescence behind me, I think I know a lot more. And I can share that with you in the following pages, all delivered with a sense of humor. I hope it helps you have a **GOOD TIME**. And that you enjoy enjoying sex!

LET'S GET STARTED

To really get into this book, all you need is a willingness to talk about sex. Yes, talk about it, because, although it's written down, I hope these lessons will be a kind of chat BETWEEN ME AND YOU. A conversation where we talk long and hard about sex, and we won't mince our words.

What's this book about? ☺

Everything to do with sex. **FROM THE INITIAL** sexual awakening to the act of sex, and all the stages in between. We'll also talk about the intimate relationship that every person has with their own body, about your first steps as part of a couple... and what comes next! **IT'S A WHISTLE-STOP TOUR** with information that will make you familiar with sex.

It's important for you to understand that I'm **NOT** going to tell you whether you should be practicing sex or not. This is up to you. What I will tell you is what you need to know if you do end up having sex, and how to be prepared for it.

The table of contents gives you each chapter title and it will help you get an idea of what each section's about. At the end of the book you'll find a glossary with useful definitions!

Who is this book for?

For curious, mature people who want to be **WELL INFORMED**. You can start to learn about sex and explore your sexuality without having sexual intercourse, and it's important to be totally clued in when it is the right time. When that time comes, the most important thing is to do it safely and consensually.

GO FOR IT!
↓

DON'T READ
THIS BOOK IF...

You don't like talking
about sex.

You have prejudices.

You don't like calling things
by their name.

Thinking about sex makes
you feel sick.

READ THIS
BOOK IF...

You want to know
everything about sex.

You don't have prejudices.

You like calling things
by their name.

The more you learn, the
more excited you feel.

☺ Did you know . . . ?

We all have that one obsessive crush. I'll tell you a LITTLE SECRET: when I was a teenager I was head over heels in love with Nick Carter, one of the Backstreet Boys. I had a life-size poster of him in my bedroom, and I kissed it so much that the face wore away!

What will you find here?

Explanations, descriptions, ideas, stories, urban myths, interesting facts, and **ADVICE**. I've also included some of the questions you've sent to me and said what I would do in your situation. There are a few quizzes that you can take to discover where you are and how hot you're feeling. There are also **MANY EXAMPLES OF SITUATIONS** you could easily find yourself in after you become sexually active.

Instructions for use

You can try to read this book like you would any other, starting at the beginning and working your way through to the end. You can have a quick glance at the different sections and **ALLOW YOURSELF TO BE SEDUCED**, first by the fun quizzes, the alluring images, or the shameless comic strips, and then later go into the text itself, beginning with the simpler parts, and then delving deeper. You can also use it as a guide or manual, to get answers to specific questions, or to plan your sexual future using this information. Use it however you want to. But whatever you do,

ENJOY IT!

If I'd had this book, I wouldn't have had to deal with certain problems...like not knowing how to put on a condom!

QUIZ

HOW MUCH DO YOU KNOW ABOUT SEX?

Sometimes you feel like you know everything, and other times you feel like you have absolutely no idea. What level are you at? Do this quiz, add up the results, and give yourself a grade!

You know that the clitoris . . .

* The clito . . . what? Don't ask me!

** Exists, but it sounds made up!

*** You know where to find it, and what to do with it!

You know that the foreskin . . .

* The fore . . . what? Don't ask me!

** Exists, moves around, and more!

*** You know where to find it, and what to do with it!

You think masturbation is . . .

* For sex addicts.

** A good way to let off some steam.

*** Healthy, enjoyable, and highly recommended.

Making out with someone is . . .

* Kissing a bit.

** The start of something more intense.

*** A really nice experience!

A condom is used to . . .

* Joke and mess around with your friends.

** Stop pregnancy.

*** Enjoy your sexuality in a healthy way.

Oral sex is . . .

* Where you talk instead of doing other things.

** An activity that makes you see stars.

*** When you use your mouth to give and receive pleasure.

Sex in a relationship should be . . .

* Unforgettably amazing.

** Thought about seriously.

*** Consensual and enjoyable for both partners.

¿?

RESULTS

(Between 7 and 10 *)
You're clueless!
You're either completely uninterested, or you're very confused. Now you should really get into this book, and don't skip a single page!

(Between 11 and 14 *)
Bits here and there
This stuff is ringing a bell— maybe you heard it in biology class? However, you're still unsure about a few things. What are you waiting for? If you want to tackle your uncertainty, this is your book!

(Between 15 and 18 *)
You've hit the ground running
It seems like you have a good idea what you're talking about. Although to get better in practice . . . you could do with some more theory! The lessons in this book will help solidify your ideas.

(Between 19 and 21 *)
You know your stuff!
You're well versed, but even so . . . are you sure you know it all? In this book you'll find ideas and techniques that you never even knew existed!

DISCOVER YOURSELF

There's a time in life when everything about your body changes—all thanks to adolescence. Parts that you'd hardly noticed before start to develop; acne and hair start sprouting all over; your hormones go wild . . . **DON'T BE SCARED**! This is normal and it happens to everyone.

Delicate as a flower and shaking like a leaf

The physical changes your body undergoes also come with changes in your reactions and emotions. Sometimes you'll feel extremely sensitive and want to cry at the drop of a hat; sometimes you'll feel irritable, or start laughing for no apparent reason. You'll constantly feel like a **WHIRLING TORNADO**.

Physically, you'll experience **SENSATIONS** you'd barely ever felt before. When you talk to someone you like, you might get short of breath, look down at the ground, and often you'll be barely able to speak. The gentlest touch can send shivers down your body and set your imagination running wild.

You and your reflection

If you've never been curious about yourself before, **NOW'S THE TIME**. Look at yourself in the mirror and inspect the shape of your naked body by looking and touching. Explore all its hidden nooks and crannies. Knowing your body is where sex begins.

At first, you might be embarrassed or feel like the image in the mirror isn't what you'd like it to be. **STOP JUDGING YOURSELF**. Don't trust in images of ideal beauty; they change all the time. Feeling good in your own skin increases attractiveness, and those around you will pick up on this.

The more you enjoy your own body, the more beautiful and attractive you'll find it. **SIZE MEANS NOTHING**: not for penises, not for boobs, not for anything. The important thing is to know your body and know how to use it; this will help you to **SATISFY YOURSELF** in a relationship.

Love your own body and let it be your guide to **A WORLD OF NEW SENSATIONS**.

MYTHS AND MISCONCEPTIONS

CHUSITA tells the truth

"The bigger a guy's penis is, the more pleasure his partner will experience."

NOT AT ALL! A big penis does not mean more pleasure. The most important thing is to know how to use what you've got.

"Girls don't care about the physical."

UM, NOOOO. Of course they do, just like everyone else! But this doesn't mean that they only care about what they see, because the feelings that develop through your other senses are more important.

"If a guy has big feet (or long fingers or arms), it means he has a big penis."

FALSE. No one body part can determine the size of another.

"Boys are constantly thinking about sex."

THINK SO? If they did, they would never get anything done. And girls do think about it, too. No one spends *all* their time thinking about sex.

"You have to shave to be beautiful."

DON'T EVEN START! Where there is hair, there is pleasure! Pubic hair is there for a reason. Wear it the way you feel most comfortable.

"Boys who can't grow beards are underdeveloped."

COME ON! There's no set age for when you should get a beard or mustache, and they don't have anything to do with someone's emotional or sexual development.

"People only like girls with big boobs."

YOU SURE ABOUT THAT? Big boobs might catch attention, of course . . . But someone can like a girl for lots of reasons, not just because of her chest size. And many people like all different sizes of boobs.

Size and girth don't matter—the important thing is what you do with it.

BY CHUSITA

FEMALE BODIES

Your figure has grown bigger and filled out, and your hips have widened (along with your butt), your waist is changing, your breasts have grown, your nipples are more noticeable, and you've probably started your period ... All of these things mean that your body is now developed. Be careful! You're now able to reproduce. **GULP.** Be sure to take precautions.

New sensations

With so many new changes, it's not surprising that you feel confused. You get emotional much more easily and you start to feel attracted to others. It's an attraction that is deeper than a crush on your favorite singer or actor. It's your **SEXUAL AWAKENING,** and there's no reason to be scared or embarrassed by it.

Your body has started producing the hormones responsible for your physical and emotional changes, as well as an increased **LIBIDO**, otherwise known as sex drive.

You'll experience a mixture of feelings and sexual thoughts, including erotic fantasies ...

Your **FIRST EXPERIENCES** will probably be with yourself, so it's important to get to know your body, because your genitals have changed both in their size and in the way they function.

SEX GUIDES suggest that you use a mirror to get a good look at your vagina. Do it! You'll find that what you see is nothing like the pictures in textbooks, which are oversimplified. Human nature is quite a bit ... **REALER** than that!

Explore your body

MONS VENERIS OR PUBIS: The triangle-shaped area of flesh between the legs, which is normally covered in a thick layer of hair. Stroking it helps you become aroused.

LABIA MAJORA: The folds that surround the outside of the vulva. When you become aroused, these separate.

LABIA MINORA: The interior folds of the vagina, which are full of nerve endings; this makes them very sensitive. They join at the top, covering the clitoris. During arousal, they increase in size.

CLITORIS: A small organ above the vaginal opening, which is extremely sensitive. When it's stimulated, it becomes erect.

VAGINAL OPENING: It's the larger opening situated below the urethra. When you are aroused, it will become moist and widen to allow penetration.

VULVA: This is all the external genitals of the female body, including the labia and the clitoris.

Bodies and identities don't always match

Everyone has a gender identity, and sometimes a person's body doesn't align with their gender identity. Thinking about and questioning gender identity are part of understanding who you are. No matter what, you might benefit from reading about female bodies and male bodies, and for more information about transgender identity, see page 44.

Beauty issues

Don't even think about googling a "normal-looking" vagina because **EVERYONE IS DIFFERENT**. Some have a more or less pronounced pubis, others have larger labia . . . and if there's hair, it's there for a reason! Hair protects your most sensitive areas from bacteria and even increases sensitivity during sex.

There's no point in trying to have a perfect body. What's most important is to **FEEL COMFORTABLE** in your own skin. If you do want to change your body, do it in a controlled way, with healthy eating and exercise, or with the help of a professional. It's totally okay to **DECORATE YOUR BODY** with a few embellishments here and there, but it's not a bad idea to stick to things that you can remove later. You have your whole life to decide if you want something that will stay forever.

Breasts and nipples

There is a common **FEMALE OBSESSION** surrounding breasts and their size, because we tend to think that big boobs will make us attractive. Forget about comparing sizes and firmness. Who cares about the color of your areola? Dark brown or

Sexual awakening is normal. Don't be scared or embarrassed by it. BY CHUSITA

light pink or anywhere in between is great. And don't worry about the size of the areola either; it's not too big or too small, and it changes depending on if you're hot or cold anyway! Your boobs, whatever they look like, are incredible. Get to know and enjoy them. Breasts, and especially nipples, **ARE HIGHLY SENSITIVE** and you can have a great time touching them.

The nipple is an important **PLEASURE POINT**, and when stimulated it stands up and hardens. However, some nipples do not respond to arousal, and there are times when stimulation just causes irritation. Every person has a different level of sensitivity, and this also varies depending on where you are in your cycle. Nipples normally become inflamed and irritable a few days before your period. As you come to know yourself better, you'll know what's normal for you.

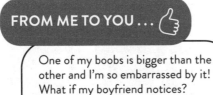

FROM ME TO YOU . . .

One of my boobs is bigger than the other and I'm so embarrassed by it! What if my boyfriend notices?
I. P., 14

Don't be surprised or worried—what you're experiencing IS NORMAL! Lots of girls find that one breast grows more quickly than the other at first, and it often equals out. In any case, remember that very few bodies are actually symmetrical. It's very common for boys, for example, to have one testicle that's bigger than the other. **CHUSITA**

Your own pace

You're the one who gets to decide how much importance to place on your first experiences, in line with your own values. In the past, "virginity" was like a prized possession, and now it can sometimes seem like it's a race to see who can be the first to lose it. But come on! Neither one belief nor the other is completely true.

Sex as part of a relationship is not the only way to **EXPERIENCE SEXUALITY**. You can experience it in whichever way you like; there's no need to be in a relationship if you don't feel ready or you don't want to be. You can just kiss and cuddle the person you like, you can just masturbate . . . Don't try to rush a sexual connection, because **FEELINGS COME AT THEIR OWN PACE**; it might be sooner or it might be later. You have a long time ahead of you to start having sexual experiences at your own pace.

The hymen

If there is a part of your body linked to your virginity, it's the hymen. But you don't have to think of it as a flower that you give to somebody; your hymen **IS JUST ANOTHER PART OF YOUR BODY**.

The hymen is a thin membrane of tissue that is located *around* the vaginal opening—not *over* it, as some people believe. It also doesn't "break," though it may tear when you first experience penetrative sex, which can produce minimal blood. But it won't always happen like that! Many girls don't even notice that their hymen has torn, either because there wasn't much

tissue there to begin with—or because it bleeds days later.

It doesn't normally break during masturbation either, or when using a tampon, or during exercise—although sometimes it can tear. It could be that the hymen doesn't completely break during your first time.

DON'T WORRY. If or when it breaks, it's not dangerous.

Slang

Breasts
boobs · puppies · cans
rack · jugs
bust · tits · titties

Vagina
twat
pussy · lady garden
beaver
cooch
bearded clam
vajayjay

Clitoris
clit · nub · love bud
bean
pearl · sweet spot
button

Menstruation
crimson tide · period
on the rag
time of the month · Aunt Flo
lady business

Buttocks
junk · buns
can · money maker
booty
fanny · tushy

MALE BODIES ♂

One day you will find, unexpectedly, that your penis **HAS SUDDENLY GROWN**. It's no longer just the organ you pee with . . . and it starts to have a life of its own! Your hormones go wild, you experience sudden **SEXUAL IMPULSES** when you see a suggestive image, and unexpected feelings rush through the most intimate parts of your body.

If you wake up to find your sheets and pajamas messy, don't worry. It's natural to start having **WET DREAMS** when puberty begins, as you're constantly producing sperm and it needs somewhere to go. Your body is developing—but be careful! You're now able to reproduce. **GULP!** Be sure to take precautions.

THIS IS NOT THE ONLY CHANGE: your testicles have also grown and they will continue to grow, just like your penis, until you are about eighteen years old. You might also start to grow a beard and mustache, your voice will change, and your muscles will feel stronger.

This is the time to inspect yourself and get to know your genitals without judging them. It could be that one testicle is bigger than the other, or it might hang lower, giving the appearance that it's sagging. **THIS IS NORMAL.** As you grow, everything will often start to equal out and move into its correct place.

The penis will no longer stay flaccid, and **YOU WILL GET ERECTIONS** several times a day. They can happen on their own, especially when you wake up, or you can make them happen by stimulating yourself. You may also notice a whitish secretion when you separate the foreskin from the glans. This is called smegma and you should remove it by carefully cleaning yourself with water.

FROM ME TO YOU . . . 👍

My penis is not very big, even when it's erect. I heard that using it a lot helps it to grow. Is that true?
J. J., 15

No! You can't build it up with exercise, because it's not a muscle. However, it may continue to grow by itself for a few more years, until it reaches its full adult size. **CHUSITA**

Sometimes you just can't help comparing your genitals with others', whether it's in the changing room, at the gym showers, or in public restrooms. **DON'T BECOME OBSESSED BY IT!** The most important thing is to know your own body well and get comfortable with it.

Arousal, which can happen when you least expect it, has probably already led you to touch your own genitals. And if you still haven't tried touching yourself, get ready to. Masturbation is **HEALTHY AND NATURAL**. I even have an entire chapter dedicated to it.

Explore your body ✍

SHAFT: The longest part of the penis, which hardens and grows during an erection.

FORESKIN: The skin that covers the glans, which may be removed via circumcision. It is connected to the glans by the frenum, a ligament that usually slides backward during an erection.

GLANS: This is the upper and most sensitive part of your penis. During arousal, it is exposed and becomes even more sensitive.

URETHRA: This is the hole where urine and semen come out. During an erection, it widens.

TESTICLES AND SCROTUM: Testicles are the glands that produce sperm. When stimulated, they rise and enlarge. The outer sac that covers them is the scrotum, tissue that is very sensitive to touch.

PERINEUM: An area located between the testicles and the anus, it's highly sensitive and comfortable to stroke. Some people say this area covers the male G-spot, or prostate.

ANUS: It is very sensitive and will sometimes contract when you are aroused. Contractions can be intensified with stimulation.

SEMEN OR SPERM: The viscous liquid produced by the testicles and released through the urethra during orgasm, when you ejaculate.

Types of erection

When a guy becomes aroused, blood is redirected to the penis, which increases in size and girth and hardens, producing an erection. This is a natural response to **REAL OR IMAGINARY STIMULATION**, and as you get to know your body you'll be able to control it more. It may only last a few seconds, softening or even disappearing suddenly. Or it can last for up to half an hour with stimulation.

Every man experiences erections differently and there is no typical erection. Your penis may point upward, downward, or directly in front of you, or **CHANGE ITS DIRECTION** depending on how turned on you are.

Sometimes, especially during adolescence, boys experience **SPONTANEOUS AND INVOLUNTARY** erections. If this happens at an intimate moment it doesn't matter too much, and at home alone you can let yourself get carried away with those feelings of arousal.

Problems tend to happen when you get an erection in public, or at an inconvenient time. It's normal to want to suppress or conceal it, but there's no reason to be embarrassed. In any case, **DON'T BE UPSET BY IT**; it happens to every guy at some point or another. Breathe deeply, and think about something nonsexual that will cool you down. This is all part of discovering your own body.

As you get to know yourself, you will learn how to heighten your arousal, and how to stop it when the moment's not right.

If at any point you want an erection but can't get one, respond calmly, and try to keep a sense of humor. If it doesn't happen now, it will happen later. It's probably only a **MENTAL BLOCK**, brought on by the pressure to perform. When you relax, you'll often have absolutely no problem getting an erection. If you are still concerned, don't hesitate to consult a doctor or counselor.

Size issues

If there's one thing that every guy worries about, it's his **PENIS SIZE**. You can all calm down! Every penis is different and there's no guide that tells us which is best. Any penis is great if you know how to use it. When pleasing someone else sexually, size means nothing. What's more, a penis that's too large can actually be uncomfortable for your partner. And anyway, there are other ways to please your partner—using your hands, your mouth, your words . . .

A normal penis size ranges from about 3 to 4 inches when it is flaccid, with an average of about 3.5, and when erect it grows to between 5 and 7 inches, with an average of about 5.5. If you've ever heard that old rumor about the 12-inch-long schlong . . .

NOT TRUE!

Beyond your penis

Male genitals are made up of more than just your penis and testicles. Don't forget your **PERINEUM**, the area between the scrotum and anus. Don't be embarrassed to touch it, or stimulate it in different ways—there's intense pleasure to be had there.

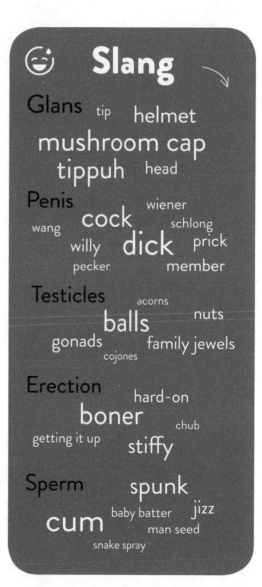

Slang

Glans tip helmet
mushroom cap
tippuh head

Penis wiener
wang cock schlong
willy dick prick
pecker member

Testicles acorns
balls nuts
gonads family jewels
cojones

Erection hard-on
boner chub
getting it up stiffy

Sperm spunk
cum baby batter jizz
man seed
snake spray

PLEASURE

When your body becomes sexually excited and is stimulated, you feel sexual pleasure. When you first discover this feeling, it's a very intense bodily experience. Pleasure lifts your mood and makes you feel satisfied and happier with yourself. Giving and receiving it is **TRULY AN ART**!

Every person has different sexual feelings, and pleasure can change with each moment and with every opportunity. Don't confuse pleasure with having an orgasm, because they're not the same thing and they don't always happen together. There are different levels of pleasure and stages you pass through to achieve more intense sexual feelings, until, finally, beginning to climax and perhaps having an orgasm. You should also know that pleasure **GETS BETTER WITH EXPERIENCE**.

You can become aroused in different ways, even just from thoughts or dreams. It's dependent on a number of factors, such as where you are, who you're with, or even your mood or your state of health. Pleasure **IS NOT AN EXACT SCIENCE**, and what had you hanging from the rafters before might not do anything for you next time. But it's worth mentioning: there's **NO PRESSURE** to spare your partner's feelings. Don't pretend you're enjoying something for their sake, and don't stress yourself out if it's not working for you—sometimes it's just not the right time, and

you're not in the right mood. That's okay! The key is to be kind, gentle, and honest with your partner.

Erotic fantasies

When you're alone, one of the most interesting sexual experiences is to use your imagination. This means relaxing and allowing yourself to be carried away by sexual thoughts. You can create **YOUR OWN EROTIC EXPERIENCES**, choosing whoever you feel drawn to. Try sexual games that turn you on! (You'll hear about those a bit later, in the chapter titled "Masturbation.")

Two-player games

When you're with somebody you like and trust, you'll discover new **STAGES AND INTENSITIES** of pleasure with them. From holding hands to the very first kiss, right up to touching each other and making love, there's a whole symphony of moments for you to enjoy and take immense pleasure in.

In a couple, the only rule is that **BOTH OF YOU SHOULD ENJOY** whatever it is you do. It's best never to force things and to allow pleasure to come naturally.

Take your time

In order to know what you find most pleasurable, you need to experiment with yourself. Discovering your own body isn't just about knowing what it's like, it's also about recognizing sensation, where you feel more intensely, what you like best, and what you don't like . . . and all of this **TAKES TIME**.

Movies, TV, many novels, and what we see in everyday life make it look like sex is always incredible. Sex is healthy and definitely pleasurable . . . **BUT DON'T ROMANTICIZE IT!** Not all relationships are wonderful, and people are not always comfortable with or up for everything.

Pleasure is found along a path taken slowly, with patience and appreciation for the journey itself. Don't force yourself to do something you don't want to, and **RESPECT THE LIMITATIONS** of your body and, of course, your partner's body. If now's not the time . . . it's okay to wait!

INTERESTING FACTS ☺

In the animal kingdom: Humans are not the only living creatures who have sex for reasons other than reproduction: bonobos and dolphins are two types of animals that have sex for pleasure.

In the *Guinness World Records* book: The man with the world's largest penis (over 19 inches!) is from Mexico. His size doesn't make him happy, and he actually considers it a handicap.

In movies: In the rom-com *When Harry Met Sally . . .*, Sally explains to Harry that women are experts in faking pleasure, and proceeds to fake an orgasm—in the middle of a restaurant!

In philosophy: Hedonism is an ancient Greek doctrine that considers pleasure to be the essence, and the only true purpose, of living. So hedonists are people who seek only joy in life, shunning all else.

In history: Sodom and Gomorrah were two ancient cities whose inhabitants gave themselves completely over to carnal pleasures. For this reason, they were struck with divine wrath from above.

FROM ME TO YOU . . . 👍

When I masturbate, I never get to orgasm, because I always ejaculate before climaxing. Am I a freak? **A. G., 14**

Not at all. Don't worry about it, just relax. Especially at first, it's common for boys to ejaculate without experiencing pleasure, and it's something you'll be able to control with time. **CHUSITA**

Using all five senses

Pleasure can be sought in all kinds of ways by using all the senses. Do you dare to try?

SIGHT: Contemplating the person you desire, exploring what you can already see, and discovering the parts that are usually hidden is an erotic game that can be very gratifying. From those first seductive gazes, it's a world of possibilities!

SOUND: Flirting, whispering dirty words in someone's ear, or even just sitting in silence with the person you like and listening to their breathing feels pretty hot! And if there's a song playing in the background, what more could you ask?

SMELL: You were probably attracted to the smell of your partner before you even realized it. Those are pheromones for you! Pheromones give off a natural odor, almost imperceptible, that sends out sex signals to attract others. For this reason, while keeping clean, you should try not to overuse perfumes or deodorant, as they can block your natural scent.

TOUCH: The art of touching and letting yourself be touched is about more than putting this hand here and that hand there. First, use one fingertip, then two or three, your whole hand, and then both hands, alternately stroking and massaging, noticing hairs bristle as you do. Playing this game is highly erotic and full of pleasure!

TASTE: Mouths are for more than smiling and seduction. Tasting your partner by kissing them is highly pleasurable and something you just have to try! However, the mouth is not the only body part you can taste. You can also try the neck, shoulders, and, what the heck, every corner of the body!

☞ Everything has its time

Sex should be **PLEASURABLE**. If it's not, because of discomfort or pain (physical or mental), it's probably best to wait and leave it for another day.

THE FEMALE ORGASM ♀

An orgasm is thought of as the pinnacle of sexual pleasure, a moment of ecstasy. However, **GETTING TO A CLIMAX** isn't always easy. The best ones don't come right away; they build up through a process of stimulation that involves the mind just as much as the body.

You probably won't reach an orgasm the first time you have sex or even when you begin to masturbate. The best way to achieve an orgasm is to know yourself, know which parts of your body are most sensitive and responsive, and know **HOW TO ACTIVATE THEM**.

Pleasure points

There are **MANY POINTS** in the female genitals capable of giving pleasure! One of these is the clitoris, and many girls reach orgasm purely by stimulating it. The vagina, when stimulated by rubbing or close contact, is another place that is most able to produce an orgasm. Some people also refer to the G-spot, an area sexologists place at about 2 to 3 inches deep, in the frontal wall of the vagina, although not all girls need to find it. An orgasm can be produced by stimulating the clitoris, the vagina, or both at the same time.

Sexual intercourse isn't the only way to have an orgasm; it can also be achieved by masturbating and with foreplay. Sometimes, you can only orgasm if you fantasize or when other parts of your body

How to recognize an orgasm

- You experience an intense feeling of pleasure in and around your genitals, which feels like palpitations or contractions.
- Your heartbeat and breathing become accelerated.
- It usually lasts between six and thirty seconds, although it can be prolonged for up to a whole minute.

are stimulated during sex. Every woman has **DIFFERENT ORGASMS** and one woman might experience different types of orgasms depending on the partner and the situation she's in.

It's not that easy, and doesn't tend to happen the first few times you try, but it is possible to have a second orgasm . . . and perhaps even more! Women who experience this are called "multi-orgasmic."

Do girls ejaculate?

Many people believe that girls only experience dry orgasms. However, that is not always the case. I'll start by saying that **EVERYBODY** produces a certain amount of sexual fluid. In addition to this, some girls produce a clear liquid, different from urine, when they orgasm. If this happens to you, **STAY CALM**! This is called female ejaculation, and it is a part of your pleasure.

If you ejaculate while masturbating, it will probably happen when you reach orgasm with somebody else, too. **DON'T BE EMBARRASSED BY IT**, because you should really feel quite the opposite. Just think, there are lots of girls who try to ejaculate and can never manage it. It could also never happen to you in your life, until it does one day—no two orgasms are the same!

Fact . . . or fiction?!

The preconception that every sexual experience between partners has to end in a shared orgasm means that some girls end up faking something they don't really feel. Sometimes they only do it to please their partner. Some girls say they fake it to try to trick themselves into climaxing, stimulating themselves so they can orgasm that way. Know that there is no need to fake an orgasm. Just **TRY TO BE YOURSELF** and act the way you feel. If you're with a partner who climaxes before you do, there's no need to end it there; ask them to come along for the ride until you orgasm, too.

THE MALE ORGASM

It might seem like the male orgasm holds no secrets, but are we really sure about that? Not all guys are the same, and not all orgasms are as straightforward as they appear. It's best to know yourself, take your time, and enjoy the journey. This way you will have even **MORE PLEASURABLE** orgasms.

The male orgasm is generally associated with ejaculation, although these two things do not always happen at the same time. Most men ejaculate when they experience an orgasm, but **IT VARIES**.

Sometimes you can climax without being able to ejaculate. The body feels that explosive sensation of pleasure and, when the moment passes, you lose the erection. Although it sounds like a myth, **ORGASMS WITHOUT SEMEN** are more common than you would think. Or you may be able to maintain an erection and go on to have **SEVERAL ORGASMS**, although this is less common.

☺ Did you know . . . ?

Around 10 to 15 million sperm are released during ejaculation. They can travel 6 to 8 inches at around 30 mph!

If you are anxious or stressed, you may find that you ejaculate without experiencing the amount of pleasure you were hoping to as you begin to climax or just before reaching orgasm. When this happens, try to relax and **DON'T GET FRUSTRATED**! Practice and experience are the best cures for this particular problem. And if you still want to continue after ejaculation, you can experience arousal by stimulating different parts of your body, which will help you climax again.

Other pleasure points

The penis is not the only part of your body that can experience pleasure. Your orgasm is usually much more intense when your testicles are stroked at the same time . . . and when you explore even **FARTHER BEHIND**!

One of the most sensitive male pleasure points, and also one of the least well known, is the male G-spot, otherwise known as the prostate. It's the gland that produces seminal fluid, located in front of the rectum, and it is **EXTREMELY SENSITIVE**! It can be stimulated externally by massaging between the scrotum and the anus, as well as internally, with your fingers. . . . This is most definitely not taboo!

Delaying ejaculation

With practice, you can learn to hold off ejaculation, which will help you experience a more pleasurable orgasm later. To do this, you need to **RECOGNIZE WHEN YOU BEGIN TO CLIMAX**. The sensations that precede an orgasm are muscle contractions and accelerated heartbeat and breathing.

Slowing down the rhythm, changing position, breathing deeply, and calming your thoughts will help you **LAST LONGER** without losing the erection.

When semen is finally released, the penis loses its stiffness. The time between losing and gaining an erection can be anything between 5 minutes and several hours, depending on the guy, but this "recovery" period can be shortened with practice.

ATTRACTION AND GENDER

Before reading this chapter, I recommend that you **RID YOURSELF OF ANY PRE-CONCEPTIONS** about masculinity and femininity.

GENDER IDENTITY is a private thing, and it doesn't help to understand it as conditioned by external factors. Sometimes, your gender identity aligns with your genitals, although it doesn't always happen this way. Some people assigned male at birth identify as women, and some people assigned female at birth identify as men.

Sexual orientation

We also have an individual **SEXUAL ORIENTATION**, which is revealed through physical attraction to others, either of the same sex or not. This is not something you can choose; it is innate. Going against what you feel is very difficult, as well as being completely unnecessary. You can perceive your sexual inclinations by listening to your thoughts and fantasies, and these will arise naturally.

People who are attracted to a different gender are called **HETEROSEXUAL**, or straight; those who are attracted to the same sex are called **HOMOSEXUAL**, or gay (men and women), or lesbians (just women); those who are attracted to both men and women are called **BISEXUAL**, and those who are attracted to all types of genders are called **PANSEXUAL**.

And, as you will see on pages 44–45, there are **EVEN MORE LABELS** than this, so don't get too bogged down in them. **TAKE YOUR TIME.** Don't let yourself be forced into certain roles, or change how you act to fit in with others' expectations, because you are the best qualified to define yourself.

☞ Take note!

LGBTQAI stands for "lesbian, gay, bisexual, trans, queer or questioning, asexual, and intersex." It is often used in its shortened form **LGBT** or written in other variants.

MYTHS AND MISCONCEPTIONS

CHUSITA tells the truth

"Being gay is a disease."

NOT TRUE! The only people who are sick are the ones still spouting this kind of bullshit in the 21st century. Homosexuality is a sexual orientation and has nothing to do with your health.

"Feminine boys are gay, and masculine girls are lesbians."

UH, REALLY? Neither of those things is true. Physical appearance, likes/dislikes, or hobbies have nothing to do with someone's sexuality. The only thing that defines your orientation is who you're attracted to, and it doesn't matter what gender they are.

"You're gay if you kissed kids of the same sex for fun when you were younger."

FALSE. All children like kissing their friends. They don't care about the gender; they're just experimenting. This is not related to sexual orientation!

"Only feminine boys cry."

WHAAAT??? Right, let's see . . . so only women are allowed to cry?! Every person needs to cry, some more than others. Gender has nothing to do with it!

"Lesbians are weird and hate men."

ABSOLUTELY NOT! This is just another stupid prejudice. A gay girl is no more or less strange than a straight girl, and sexual orientation has nothing to do with liking or disliking people based on their gender.

"You have to be really good-looking for people to be interested in you."

YOU'RE KIDDING ME! Not likely! If people were only attracted to supermodels, what would the rest of us be doing right now?

During adolescence, it's normal to experiment with different types of relationships. Learn from them!

Attraction and emotions

Not everybody is attracted to the same kind of person...thankfully! All of our senses are involved in feelings of attraction. **YOU HAVE TO PAY ATTENTION TO THEM!**

When you're attracted to someone, **IT TURNS YOUR WHOLE WORLD UPSIDE DOWN**! You want to be close to them, touch them, and be touched by them. It's a kind of magnetism, which affects your body and your mind, but it doesn't always develop into love! Attraction can hit you when you least expect it. The important thing is that you can **FIND WHAT YOU LIKE AND ACCEPT IT**.

Open your mind!

Romantic and physical attraction toward another person will help you know your sexual orientation, although this can change with time. . . . Accept yourself as you are, and respect others' choices, too.

INTERESTING FACTS 😮

In music: The Austrian singer Conchita Wurst was the first bearded woman to be entered into, and go on to win, the Eurovision Song Contest, smashing preconceptions about gender along the way.

In the press: Cara Delevingne and Lily-Rose Depp are just two of many celebrities who have stated that they are bisexual.

In the theater: The cult comedy *Priscilla, Queen of the Desert* brought drag to mainstream audiences in the nineties. The story has now become a successful musical which sells out in theaters around the world.

In movies: *Blue Is the Warmest Color* follows the sexual awakening of a teenager who falls for another girl. It is now a cult film.

In the animal kingdom: Homosexuality is not exclusive to humans. Homosexual behavior has been identified in over 1,500 species, from insects to mammals.

☞ Take note!

If your sexual preferences mean you are not accepted, look for support. There are relatives and friends, as well as LGBTQAI groups, waiting for you with open arms. And if you do come across homophobic attitudes or experience abuse because of your sexuality, **REPORT IT.**

STRAIGHT

You're attracted to people of **ANOTHER GENDER**. This is a commonly accepted sexuality in most societies. Even though many people doubt their heterosexuality, it is often taken for granted that someone is straight. Listen to yourself and don't be scared. Everyone has doubts sometimes, whatever their sexual orientation.

When you start to mature sexually, **YOU MIGHT BE TURNED ON** for many reasons by a man or a woman, but this doesn't mean anything. The real relationships that you establish with others are what determine your orientation.

In boy-girl relationships, there is no need to fall into **OUTDATED GENDER ROLES**.

Neither gender is stronger or weaker than the other. You are just two people who have different strengths and weaknesses that change all the time.

> 👆 **Remember . . .**
>
> The prefix *hetero-* means "different" and refers to male and female genders. However, it DOESN'T mean "normal." Heterosexuality is just another sexual orientation.

Different bodies

You're attracted to a different gender, a body that is **DIFFERENT FROM YOURS**, a body that you're not familiar with. Yes, yes, we've all studied human anatomy at school, but this definitely doesn't make us experts! When you like someone, you'll notice how your feelings change, how you become aroused . . . But how does someone from another gender react and become aroused? The best way to find out is to look at things from their point of view!

We're all people!

Some people are more romantic and like to take their time, and others are more passionate and pretty much up for anything. In any case, every relationship has a different **RHYTHM AND PACE**, and when different types of bodies are involved, these aren't the only differences! All that matters is that you communicate your needs and desires with each other, and approach each other with **MUTUAL RESPECT**.

I've always thought I was straight, because I like boys and I have a boyfriend. But the other day I had a dream where I was having sex with a girl . . . and I liked it! Does this make me a lesbian?
E. G., 15

Not at all! Dreams don't say anything about a person's sexuality, they're just fantasies. This kind of thing happens to everybody at some point: straight people dream about having sex with someone of the same gender, and gay people have dreams about a different gender. It doesn't mean anything.
CHUSITA

Common beliefs and clichés

GIRLS don't have to be super sexualized and act very feminine, and **BOYS** don't have to be muscular and act macho, either. Each person can be whatever they feel like and act however they feel most comfortable, because attractions develop naturally this way.

They say that girls are more sensitive and want long-term, stable relationships. Boys, in contrast, are very superficial, only interested in as much sex as they can get. But like everything, this is not always the case. When you mature sexually, boys and girls look for both **SEX AND AFFECTION**, sometimes leaning toward the one and sometimes toward the other, depending on how intimate you are feeling.

That old belief that girls should wait for boys to **MAKE THE FIRST MOVE** is extremely old-fashioned! Of course girls can take the initiative, whether it's to ask someone on a date or for something more

sexual. In any case, you should always **RESPECT THE OTHER PERSON**.

That means not approaching someone aggressively or invading their personal space. The best approach, whatever your gender, is to test the water and even ask if that person is interested before suggesting something physical.

GAY ♀♀ ♂♂

If you're attracted to people of the **SAME SEX**, at first you might be frightened by your own feelings. There's no need to feel anxious. Being lesbian or gay is just another sexual orientation, as natural as being straight. Sometimes, depending on the company you keep, you might hear people tell jokes about being gay: don't let them embarrass you. **BE YOURSELF**. Gay people exist in every kind of society, because it is absolutely normal.

In the past, teenagers who discovered they were gay encountered many difficulties and faced discrimination, and while some still do there are now many places people are much more tolerant. **DON'T TAKE ANY NOTICE OF WHAT PEOPLE SAY**; the important thing is that you are happy. Don't try to hide your feelings, because lying to yourself will only make you unhappy.

You're not alone!

You don't need to pretend to be something you're not, or deny your sexual orientation to anyone. It's better to share, especially with the people closest to you, because it's likely that your friends, relatives, and teachers **WILL SUPPORT YOU** and give you the help you need.

Break the mold

There are no set criteria for how a gay man or woman should look or act. Guys don't need to act effeminately, and girls don't have to put on a masculine front. **GAY PEOPLE COME IN ALL EXPRESSIONS**, and there is no way to tell if someone is gay just by appearances.

And you shouldn't feel the need to reproduce heterosexual roles in a gay relationship. You know the ones we are bombarded with daily in the media, and in general life? You shouldn't feel like one of you has to take on a masculine role and the other a feminine role.

Coming out

Pretty much everyone who's come out is happy they did. That said, the people they tell don't always react well. Being true to yourself is important, and so is being safe. It's a good idea to come out to the people in your life in stages, and have a plan in case the person you're telling doesn't react the way you're hoping they will. Stay safe! Coming out to friends and trusted family members your own age first and then leaning on them for help with others is a time-tested technique.

In sync!

When you're attracted to people of the same gender, it can be hard at first to find out if someone is open to a same-sex relationship. You'll probably be overcome with doubt, not knowing if you should tiptoe around it or just dive straight in!

When you feel uncertain, there are a few recommendations it doesn't hurt to follow:

Before taking the next step . . .

- Find out if they are comfortable with LGBTQAI culture.

- See if they seem happy to have you physically close.

- Try to make them feel comfortable around you and check by asking.

- Don't become impatient or put pressure on them.

- Let them know your orientation and the fact that you are attracted to them.

- If they don't reciprocate, don't insist, because you could offend them, and the only person who will get hurt is you.

BEYOND LABELS 😎

There are ways of experiencing sexuality that go beyond straight and gay. If you feel uncertain about your sexuality, don't worry, there's no rush to label yourself. It's best not to follow rules imposed by others. Break free of their stereotypes and prejudices and, most important, **BE TRUE TO YOURSELF**. Listen to your feelings and your desires, know yourself, accept yourself, and be happy following your own sexuality.

Whatever you identify as, knowing about the different identities and sexual orientations out there can help you be comfortable with who you are.

Bisexual or pansexual

People who are attracted to both **MEN** and **WOMEN** are called "bisexual."

Sometimes people discover this about themselves gradually, through different phases. For example, someone might define themselves as straight or gay at first, and then, with time, begin to realize their attraction to more than one sex.

There are also people who identify as "pansexual", which is a broader label meaning you are not attracted to a certain gender but to individual people. Pansexuals recognize there are more than two gender identities.

Transsexual and transgender

Transgender people don't always feel like they fit the body they were born with, and transsexual people actively transition from one sex to another. Some may opt for gender affirmation surgery, while others choose not to undergo genital surgery for personal or medical reasons—though they may use a combination of other surgery or hormone treatments if they want to affirm their gender with physical changes. For transsexual and transgender people, sexual orientation can vary—just like it can with anyone.

People can be transgender in different ways, from dressing or expressing themselves differently or using different pronouns (most often "they/them" instead of "he/him" or "she/her") to taking hormones or having surgery. The term "transvestite" is old and shouldn't be used, and some people don't identify as male or female. They are often called "non-binary." Remember, it's not required to define yourself. But transgender and non-binary people should feel empowered to talk to their partners, friends, and doctors about how they feel, just as everyone should be supportive allies when people come out as transgender or non-binary.

Asexual or demisexual

Some people **HAVE A LACK OF INTEREST** in sex. This doesn't mean they'll never go on dates, because they do feel emotional and intellectual attraction. The label *demisexual* refers to people who don't feel sexually attracted toward anyone until they have formed a **STRONG BOND** with them.

A COMMITTED RELATIONSHIP

When you find yourself attracted to somebody, it's natural to hope it develops into a **COMMITTED RELATIONSHIP**. You like each other, hang out with each other, kiss each other, fool around . . . but there are lots of other stages to go through between that initial attraction and a relationship. And not all relationships end up becoming long-term.

When a relationship is just starting out **YOU DON'T NEED TO GIVE IT A NAME**. You'll find it's not often an easy thing to do, because sometimes it's hard to know if you are just having fun together or if it's something more. Only time will tell.

Expectations?

You shouldn't set your expectations too high for a relationship. Many of us have been told that the best way is love then marriage . . . but **WE'RE STILL YOUNG** and we don't have to decide right now. We should also remember not to confuse sex with committed relationships. Two people who have been in a relationship for a while aren't obligated to have sex, and two people who have just met shouldn't feel the need to refrain from sex.

Types of love

Unrequited love: One person is completely in love with the other, and the other? Completely oblivious! This is the classic tale of unrequited love.

Platonic love: Two people get along extremely well, but is there anything more? If there isn't that spark of physical attraction, maybe "just friends" is the right call.

Passionate love: The attraction is obvious, and the two bodies desire each other. This does not mean these people are mentally in sync.

Romantic love: It's clear that both will go to great lengths to be around each other. Be careful not to fantasize too much at this point!

Committed love: Attraction, companionship, and passion have resulted in moments of true intimacy. Maybe it will be a long-term thing!

MYTHS AND MISCONCEPTIONS

CHUSITA tells the truth

"Girls have to sit around and wait for their Prince Charming to appear."

I'll tell you now: HE DOESN'T EXIST. It's true that some girls choose to wait rather than go out and find him, expecting things to happen like they do in fairy tales . . . But the truth is that he'll probably never come!

"Girls like boys and boys like girls."

NOT ALWAYS! Sexual orientation isn't set in stone. Better to let people decide for themselves!

"You have to wait at least six months before doing it with your partner."

THERE ARE NO RULES! There are couples who wait longer, maybe two years or even more. In contrast, others have sex when they barely know each other.

"When you break up with your partner, you can be best friends."

CAREFULLLLL! First things first, let's be realistic here: if two people have been in a relationship and one decides to break up, the other person might still hope they'll get back together. It's better to give it a little time and then decide whether to be friends or to move on from each other completely.

"When a guy says he's had a lot of relationships he's a player, and when a girls says it she's a slut."

ABSOLUTELY NOT. Girls and guys both have the right to choose who to go out with and what kind of relationships to pursue. You shouldn't admire someone for that or criticize them either!

"When you find your other half you will feel complete."

YOU SURE ABOUT THAT? The idea that you can find your other half is another one of those stereotypes that can really damage a relationship! Everyone should feel as complete as they can in themselves, so that we can share love and new experiences with whoever we like. Only you can complete yourself.

Relationships and sex don't always go hand in hand.

BY CHUSITA

WHAT TYPE OF RELATIONSHIP IS IT?

You like somebody a lot, and it seems like they might like you too . . . Where are you at? Take this quiz, and count the hearts to find out!

When you see each other on the street . . .
- ♥ They seem shy, awkward, and look the other way.
- ♥♥ Their face lights up and they smile.
- ♥♥♥ They wink and come running right up to you.

On the phone . . .
- ♥ They don't have your number, or if they do they never call.
- ♥♥ They text occasionally, about practical things.
- ♥♥♥ They message you and call you all the time, showing how crazy they are about you.

When you meet up . . .
- ♥ You're always with friends.
- ♥♥ You're with friends, but you two spend the whole time with each other.
- ♥♥♥ You're practically joined at the hip, just the two of you.

Their friends . . .
- ♥ Don't know you.
- ♥♥ Don't mind you.
- ♥♥♥ Get along great with you.

When you change your style . . .
- ♥ They keep looking at you but say nothing.
- ♥♥ They clearly notice.
- ♥♥♥ They ask when you did it and compliment your taste.

When another person is flirting with you . . .
- ♥ They're not bothered by it.
- ♥♥ They come straight over to deal with this nuisance.
- ♥♥♥ They grab your waist and kiss you.

When you feel down and you need to talk to someone . . .
- ♥ You'd like to talk to them but you call your best friend instead.
- ♥♥ You call but they don't answer, or if they do they don't offer the help you need.
- ♥♥♥ They answer the phone right away and comfort you.

RESULTS

(Between 7 and 10 ♥)
Just getting started
Some people are more reserved—so don't get discouraged. But it sounds like you need to be the daring one!

(Between 11 and 14 ♥)
Not together, not apart
Your relationship is like waiting at the start of a roller coaster. You may like each other and maybe you've had a few good times, but nothing's happening yet!

(Between 15 and 18 ♥)
It's on
There's a great connection between you and you like each other. You both want things to go farther. Let's see who makes the first move!

(Between 19 and 21 ♥)
Make it official!
You're totally hooked on each other. What are you waiting for? Arrange to go out together!

INTERESTING FACTS

In the animal kingdom: Swans are one of many species of bird that mate for life. And seahorses are always faithful to each other. It's said that if a seahorse loses its partner, it dies of a broken heart!

In theater: Shakespeare told the story of Romeo and Juliet, two lovers in Verona who shared an impossible love and died for it. It's a classic, and has been adapted time and again for movies.

In mythology: The Greeks told tales of Narcissus, who was so handsome and irresistible that everyone who met him fell help-lessly in love. A goddess cursed him to fall in love with his own reflection, and he died waiting for it to love him back!

In philosophy: The Greek philos-opher Plato defined the ideal love as eternal, intelligent, and perfect. What was beautiful in principle has now become something completely unobtainable.

In music: The singer Britney Spears dedicated her song "Seal It with a Kiss" to "friends with benefits," those who are a little more than friends.

BEFORE . . .

I LIKE YOU 😄

To like or not to like . . . that is the question! Every relationship, no matter what it's called, starts with **THE SAME DILEMMA**. How do you know if you're 100% into someone? And how can you know if they're 100% into you, too? There will always be clues to help you find out.

Test the waters, be nice, flirt a little, and send them messages. If they respond positively, they may be into you!

— BY CHUSITA

Are you sure you like them?

Often you want to like someone so much that you end up convincing yourself that you do. All of your friends have crushes, and you want to feel those butterflies in your stomach, too. You decide on someone . . . and let yourself get carried away! But in the back of your mind, you know you're not certain. **THERE'S NO RUSH!** Try to get to know this person more, make a list of reasons why you think you like them (not just physically!), and listen to the way your body reacts when you're together.

Yes, you like them!

If there's **SOMEONE YOU'RE ATTRACTED TO**, it's obvious and you can't avoid it. You're fixated by the things they talk about, the way they dress, and how they move . . . When you're not with them, you can't stop thinking about them. When you meet them, you get butterflies in your stomach and tingles all over your body, and your heart starts racing. **YOU'RE UNDER THEIR SPELL.**

And . . . do they like you?

The first thing you'll wonder is, do they like you back? There are lots of signs that will let you know if their answer is yes or no. To begin with, test the waters, start friendly conversations, and **FLIRT A LITTLE**. Watch their responses: if they like you, they'll follow suit. If not, accept the fact that you're just friends.

> ☺ **Some advice**
>
> Don't go around telling everyone you like someone, unless you're comfortable with that someone finding out! (Or you could try telling them yourself, too!)

We like each other. What next?

You like them and you think they like you. What are you waiting for? **ARE YOU GONNA TELL THEM OR WHAT?** It's normal to feel embarrassed, but now's not the time to be shy. However, don't rush things, either, because you don't want to startle anyone. If you like each other, things will develop naturally, when you least expect them to. But if you're sure about it . . . tell them! Don't be shy, try to be honest and direct, because **IF YOU DON'T ASK, YOU DON'T GET**.

Signs! They like you if . . .

- They notice everything you do and can hardly take their eyes off you.
- They make a detour to walk home with you.
- They try to catch your attention.
- They "like" everything you post on social media.
- In a group chat, they're always first to reply when you send a message.
- They shake and act clumsy when you get close to them.

IF YOU WANTED MY ATTENTION, YOU COULD'VE SAID SO!

DATING 😆😅

If you want to meet up with someone, don't wait for them to make the first move. You'll probably be super awkward and very embarrassed, but . . . **FACE YOUR FEARS**! Suggest something simple, like going to a movie, shopping, or out for a coffee, and be yourself. If they say no, it's fine, and if they say yes, **ENJOY IT**!

It isn't about showing off to the other person, trying to be a Hollywood star—it's about showing **THE BEST OF YOU**. This means that you don't need to obsess about your physique or appearance, because the best things in everyone are their natural characteristics.

The first date

You've arranged to meet up, and you're overcome with nerves! It's normal at this point to **DOUBT EVERYTHING**. From the classic "What should I wear?" to "Will they like me?" or the inevitable "I don't know if I should go!" **RELAX**!

On a first date, try not to let your hormones control you. Be in control of yourself. Keep your goals small: holding hands in the street, gently touching their waist . . . Anything can happen on a first date, from touching, to kissing, to **WANTING TO KEEP KISSING**! Or there might not be anything

☞ Some dating tips!

- Be on time, and if you think you'll arrive late, let them know! There's nothing worse than thinking you've been stood up.
- Don't lie about yourself to impress anyone; don't try to be someone you're not. Be you!
- Don't tell all your secrets on the first date! There are things you can reveal as you get to know

someone better. Honesty is important. But TMI isn't necessary.
- Don't pressure them to do anything they seem uncomfortable about.
- Talk about things that interest you and listen to your partner. Don't try to fill every silence.
- Be friendly and try to make the other person laugh, without overdoing

it. And absolutely do not make jokes about them, or get too vulgar!
- Forget about your cell phone. No one likes to lose someone to their phone!

physical yet. The most important thing is to only do what you both really want to. Dates are about getting to know someone in a new way, to see if you really are interested in them.

After . . .

You might find that you're not as into the other person as you thought you were, and you don't want to go out again. Or the other person might feel this way about you. In both cases: **DON'T WORRY**! And don't take it to heart. There are plenty more fish in the sea, which means plenty more people to meet, date, and try things out with.

If you enjoyed it and want to meet up again . . . Don't hesitate, **LET THEM KNOW**! Second dates tend to start out like the first: sometimes neither of you can pluck up the courage to ask!

Don't expect your first date to be magical.

BY CHUSITA

GOING OUT

You've been dating, you've told people you're together, and it's already old news. You've gotten serious enough to start thinking of yourselves as a couple. **BEING WITH SOMEONE** is about letting someone share in your private thoughts and feelings, but this doesn't mean you need to be with each other 24/7. It's good if you're both able to have your own lives, as well as a shared one. A girlfriend or boyfriend should add to your life, not change it.

There are lots of types of couples: some need to show off how they feel; others act cool as a cucumber with each other. It's all okay!

Can people change?

People **ARE THE WAY THEY ARE**, better at some things and worse at others. However, you can **CHANGE BEHAVIORS** and attitudes that bother your partner. For example, if your girlfriend/boyfriend is particularly aggressive or competitive toward you, they should change the way they speak to **MAKE YOU COMFORTABLE**. And if they don't, leave them!

Sex . . .

Being in a couple doesn't mean having sex from day one. **NOT AT ALL!** It also doesn't mean that you shouldn't, as long as you both want to, you've agreed to do it, and found the right time and place! You have the right to decide what you do and when you do it, without forcing anything.

Jealousy!

A relationship is a type of commitment that carries an unwritten rule: **FIDELITY**. If you're together, normally you wouldn't need to be with anybody else. But you could also decide on an open relationship. In an open relationship, partners can be free to see other people—but it's important to clearly communicate and be fair to everyone's needs. It's up to you! In any case, jealousy often rears its ugly head. **CAREFUL!** It's never an excuse to behave unkindly!

🔒 Rules

- Always respect your partner's privacy, and ask them to respect yours.

- Don't spy on your partner's cell phone, or let them look through yours if you don't want them to. That's invasive!

- It's a free, consensual relationship between equals. No one has power over the other!

- Don't lose friends because you have a partner. It's normal to go out together, but go out separately, too!

FROM ME TO YOU . . . 👍

I've been going out with someone for a month and they want me to send them nude photos. What should I do? **F. T., 17**

SAY NO!
Although it might seem fun and sexy now, if you break up you might regret it! (see "sexting" on p. 60.) **CHUSITA**

FRIENDS WITH BENEFITS

Sometimes there are relationships that can't be defined: you're not a couple, because you haven't made that kind of emotional connection...and you're not just friends because there's more to it than that...you're two people **WITH THE RIGHT TO MESS AROUND** every now and then: you're friends with benefits!

This is a special kind of friendship where you can kiss, touch, fool around, or have sex when you feel like it. This has **PROS AND CONS**. The good thing is there isn't the same kind of commitment as a couple. But if one person develops stronger feelings than the other, it's game over!

Rules

- You don't have to kiss every time you meet.
- You can get involved with other people or have other friends with benefits.
- If one of you isn't up for it, no one should get angry about it.
- Don't make plans or set dates with each other.
- You should both be discreet about your relationship.
- You make the rules together!

Sex...

You get to decide your level of intimacy. It's normal not to go beyond a few stolen kisses and touches the first couple of times. And you can start to **TURN UP THE HEAT** as you meet up more often. The trust you develop will mean you feel comfortable messing around, cuddling, kissing, touching more intimately...

Confusing situations

Two people who have agreed that they **DON'T** want to be in a relationship but **HOOK UP WHENEVER THEY LIKE** ... In principle it sounds great, although it's not easy to keep up! In the same way that touching creates intimacy, this type of relationship creates lots of confusion.

The relationship could end because one (or both) partners have found someone else; you stop seeing each other as often; or, with so much closeness, physical attraction develops into love. In the worst-case scenario, one of you can be in a bad position, because they fall **HOPELESSLY IN LOVE** with someone who doesn't love them back. This last issue is the most difficult to resolve, and you need to think of a solution for it as soon as possible!

Types of friends with benefits

LIFELONG FRIEND who you trust enough to mess around with and try "stuff" without worrying about commitment.

CLASSMATE who you get with every now and then, on school trips or at parties, or when you see each other at school . . . You're just another pair of friends!

ONE-NIGHT STAND AT PARTIES OR CLUBS, someone you get with when you see each other, knowing it's going to be fun!

Dealing with differences

If you fall for your friend, don't hesitate to:

- Test the waters to see if the feeling's mutual.

- Ask if they're interested in being friends with benefits, too, or if it's just you.

- Break the rules and ask to be in a real relationship.

- Break it off if they don't want the same thing. It could end up hurting you!

If you notice your friend starting to become attached and you don't reciprocate, don't give them **FALSE HOPE**! You could end up losing a friend.

HOOKUPS 😚😊

Sometimes you cross paths with someone...and Cupid strikes! It could be a complete stranger or someone you suddenly start to see in a different way, **AND YOU GET IT ON!**

Hookups are spontaneous, and can often be **VERY INTENSE**: An encounter that goes beyond a couple of kisses as you start becoming sexual...or even end up going the whole way. The only limitations are the ones you give yourselves. However, if you do have sex, use a condom! It's the only reliable contraceptive for a casual encounter.

You should try to make sure that both partners are at a similar level of **SEXUAL MATURITY** to avoid awkward situations where one of you wants to go slower or faster than the other.

Alcohol and ⚠ drugs

No judgment if this is your thing, but like everything, moderation is key—don't overdo it and drink or take more than you can handle. There might be people out there who will use alcohol or drugs as a tool to push you to do things you wouldn't normally do. They could put you in a dangerous situation, and it may be that you're too drunk or high to consent.

Stay safe. Look out for your friends and have them look out for you.

⚠ Sexting

SEXTING, the practice of sending erotic photos or messages to your partner, is dangerous because, when the relationship ends, it could result in **SEXTORTION**, a form of extortion that involves blackmailing someone with "compromising" images. An ex-partner could also publish images like these online, which is known as **REVENGE PORN**. Many people, including several celebrities, have fallen victim to these crimes by their exes.

Although nowadays everybody carries cameras around on their cell phones or tablets, it's not advisable to record yourself having sex. Your video could be shared, and end up in the wrong hands.

After . . .

It's fun to have a fling, but **BE CAREFUL**! This type of relationship can leave you vulnerable. There's zero commitment, and because of this it's the relationship that creates the most confusion.

When you hook up with someone, it's because of a mutual attraction. If you also get along well, the next day you might feel different. **DON'T GET AHEAD OF YOURSELF!** Hookups allow you to experience passion, but they don't give you much of a chance to get to know the other person. As you get to know them better, you might realize you'd prefer things not go any farther.

Rules

- Both of you have to be okay with the relationship you're going to have.

- Neither person should feel pressured to do something they don't want to, or feel obligated to continue with something they're not enjoying.

- Both of you should take responsibility for making sure you're protected. No condom, no sex.

- If you don't enjoy it, you can simply move on!

I'M BREAKING

Hooking up, being friends with benefits, going steady...No matter the type of relationship, when you're young most relationships come to **AN END**, which can sometimes be painful, and other times can be a big relief. Breaking up is **PART OF LIFE** and it's never the same, no matter how much experience you get!

Be prepared . . .

Because the relationship might come to an end, keep in mind that everything you've shared with this person could potentially be used against you, including secrets or photos, so be careful from the start.

How to leave someone

- Do it face-to-face, not by phone or text.
- Find somewhere quiet, where you will have some privacy.
- Be honest about how you feel.
- Avoid being cruel or showing resentment.
- Don't try to comfort the other person with displays of affection.

UP WITH YOU

End it!

When you're the one who puts an end to a relationship, people will think you have **THE ADVANTAGE**. It might seem easy . . . but it's not! It's good to try to end things on the best terms possible, but don't comfort them by giving out false hope. Breaking up with **NO HARD FEELINGS** is better for both of you.

When someone leaves you . . .

Knowing that the person you like, and who you've shared a relationship with, doesn't want to be with you anymore **IS HARD**. Prepare yourself: it's going to hurt. But if the other person doesn't want to continue with the relationship, it's not your fault. You will meet someone else in the future.

THE RIGHT TIME

There's a time for everything, and everything has its time. Don't force situations, or miss opportunities!

It's not always easy to find the right moment, because a lot of the time your own insecurities mean that it never happens. The most important thing is to be sure of yourself and let chemistry be your guide.

On the other hand, if you want to do something with someone . . . why are you waiting for them to make the first move? Find a moment where both of you are feeling intimate, and **TAKE THE INITIATIVE**!

The first kiss

When you decide to go for it and kiss the person you like, ask first. Don't take them by surprise—especially if you're hoping this kiss will be **THE FIRST OF MANY**. There's no instruction manual that tells you how to know when the time is right or a script that says how to do it, but there are a few mistakes you can easily avoid. For example, don't kiss someone for the first time when you're with other people, or interrupt them mid-conversation. Relax!

First sexual contact

There's no need to pounce on someone right after the first kiss and try to go farther. It's really important to have a **MUTUAL DESIRE** to move things along. And then, find an appropriate place!

Create your own perfect moment, because if you wait for it . . . you might end the date without finding it!

THE RIGHT PERSON 😚🙂

For a good relationship, even more important than the time and the place . . . is the other person! They need to respond to your advances with the same interest as you, because **NOTHING SHOULD BE FORCED**! If the other person wants to stop, you have to respect that—you have to stop.

From love to sex

When you find the right person, things might move very quickly or happen little by little. Every relationship has **ITS OWN PACE**! Don't confuse sex with love. Having crazy, passionate sex with someone doesn't mean that this person is the love of your life and, similarly, knowing you both like each other doesn't mean sex is guaranteed.

Knowing how to wait

Even if you feel like you've found the right person, your partner might not respond with the same enthusiasm. Not everyone is ready to go at the same pace. When **THEY ASK FOR MORE TIME**, you should give it. Take this news calmly, with respect, and learn to enjoy all the other things you do together. Deal with it kindly, without bitterness or pressure. Make your partner feel safe, and, little by little, they will let you know if and when they want more.

There's more to life!

Becoming sexual doesn't mean you have to have intercourse! There are many types of **FOREPLAY** to enjoy, which are also immensely pleasurable. Making out, cuddling, examining each other playfully, or even mutual masturbation are options that shouldn't be ruled out, and that can be good to suggest to the other person.

The first time

You're both sure and you go for it! But . . . don't expect fireworks! No matter how perfect the person, place, and time, the first time you get intimate is rarely as amazing as you think it'll be. It's an experience that is **WAY TOO OVER-BLOWN**. Sex is something that gets better with practice!

An unexpected treat!

You didn't expect to find the right person, or be in the right place, and you didn't think it could be the right time for both of you . . . but then it happened! Passion struck when you least expected it, and you let yourself be led by your desire. Enjoy it! **THERE'S NO REASON TO REGRET IT**, just remember to use a condom.

Knowing when to say no

After the first time, there's a second, a third, and many more. But doing something with someone once doesn't mean you have to do it again or that there should be **ANY FORM OF OBLIGATION**.

There are times when **YOU JUST HAVE TO SAY NO**. Sometimes this is a big turn-off for both of you, but it has to be done. For example, if you don't have a condom or if something just feels wrong and it stops you from continuing. **BE FIRM**: respect yourself and ask to be respected.

FROM ME TO YOU . . .

I'm going out with a girl and I'm really in love, but I'm not ready to have sex yet. She really wants it and even got undressed in front of me . . . I was so embarrassed! I don't understand what's wrong with me. Am I sick? **J. P. G., 15**

Not at all. Clearly you haven't had your moment yet. Relax about it and don't rush yourself. Explain to your girlfriend that you have different paces, and let her know how much you like her, so she doesn't think it's because you don't like her enough. **CHUSITA**

THE RIGHT PLACE

The place for intimacy **IS IMPORTANT**, because depending on where you are you'll feel more or less at ease. Clearly, if you think someone's watching you, or that they might see or hear you, you won't be able to relax! When you're a teenager it's often

☹ Where and what?

In the corner of the school grounds: It's fine to hang out, flirt, and at most share a few secret kisses or cuddles, but this place is no good for anything more. Remember you could be expelled!

At your doorway: The classic scene for your first kiss, and much more! This is a place for good-byes. It's best not to go for too long though, in case your neighbors appear, or your parents!

In the park: This is the place where most couples end up on their first dates, taking a romantic walk . . . and kissing on a bench or on the grass! You can't go much further here; anyone could walk past.

At the movies: The back row is famous for couples who want to be close . . . As long as the theater's not full! You should find a film that's not too popular, at a quiet time, but even then it's not a great place to go too far.

At a club: There are lots of people, and although the lights might mean you notice them less, it's not great to give everyone a show! Some clubs have private areas with seating but watch out for the hygiene! You're probably not the first people to have used them.

In the bathroom: The john is a good place to satiate your urges, although it leaves much to be desired in terms of hygiene. If passion strikes, enjoy it, but if the place turns you off, leave it for another time.

At the beach or in the countryside: Finding a beautiful spot in nature, secluded, and away from prying eyes . . . It's a miracle!

At home: If no one else is home, or you have plenty of privacy, this is without a doubt the best place for sexual experiments. And if you want to avoid awkward questions, leave no evidence!

harder to find the right place, because you don't have your own house or car. You have to find the right opportunity.

It wasn't the moment!

Being rejected for a kiss or sexual advance isn't the end of the world. You have to respect the other person's wishes—but make sure you talk to them. If it's not the right time for them, give them space. And if they're just not as into you as you're into them, **DON'T WORRY ABOUT IT**, there are plenty more people you'll feel attracted to—perhaps more so—and who will respond positively!

Everything's perfect . . . except you!

Sometimes everything comes together: you have privacy and a quiet place where you won't be interrupted . . . Even so, **SOMETHING'S MISSING**. Your body tells you that you don't want this. You don't need to go along with something you're not comfortable with, however perfect the situation seems. Clearly, you haven't found **YOUR MOMENT**. Don't get worked up; you can explain things calmly and say you want to stop.

PROTECTION ✋

When you start having sex, you need to be aware that it's a very pleasurable thing you can do but it also carries risks! Knowing about them is **VITAL** to practice sex safely and responsibly. Unwanted pregnancies and sexually transmitted diseases are the biggest risks you run if you don't use adequate protection.

It's important to be well informed and to understand the pros and cons of each contraceptive method, because not all methods that help you avoid pregnancy will stop you from catching sexually transmitted diseases. Protected sex will keep you safe and help you experience **HEALTHY SEXUALITY**.

Pregnancy

When a guy and a girl practice vaginal sex without protection, there's the risk that the sperm will make contact with the egg and fertilize it, causing pregnancy. Remember that the only way to prevent this is with **CONTRACEPTION**.

STIs

Sexually transmitted infections (or STIs) are illnesses transmitted through physical contact while having sex. They are caused by different viruses, bacteria, fungi, and parasites, which are passed on through bodily fluids or just from physical contact.

There are many: HIV, human papillomavirus (HPV), gonorrhea, chlamydia, genital herpes, syphilis...Some of them can be very serious or even fatal. They usually require very long treatment, sometimes for life, and they can have aftereffects. Most of them don't show symptoms right away and are difficult to detect in the short term, which makes them even more dangerous. Someone may not realize they're infected and end up passing on the disease through unprotected sex while thinking they are clean.

Diseases can be spread by intercourse—such as vaginal sex, anal sex, and oral sex—so these practices always require protection. You should also bear in mind that, if you are a teenager, you may contract these diseases more easily when exposed to them, as your immune system is still developing.

Choosing a method

Before starting to have sex, you should **ALWAYS** decide which kind of protection you will use.

This is a mutual decision that should be made before having sex. Never leave this decision solely in the other person's hands, unless you know them very well and know you can trust them. Remember, your health is at stake.

Depending on who your partner is, some methods may work better than others. At the start of any relationship, with people you don't know very well, or in one-time or spontaneous encounters, the most recommended form of protection is **A CONDOM**. It's the most common form of contraception that, as well as preventing pregnancy, also stops the spread of STIs.

When you're in a stable relationship or you trust each other a lot, it's a good idea to make sure that both of you are healthy and to rule out possible infections before using **OTHER METHODS**, which I'll tell you about later and which can be prescribed by your doctor.

Double protection

The most reliable, efficient, and recommended form of protection is the **CONDOM**: it's comfortable, practical, and, as we've mentioned, it offers double protection as it can prevent both pregnancy and STIs.

There are two types: external and internal. The **EXTERNAL CONDOM** is the most widely used and well-known: a thin layer of latex that is placed over the erect penis before sex, after which semen is held in the tip. The **INTERNAL CONDOM**, often made of polyurethane, has a ring that should be placed over the vulva, and another smaller ring on the opposite end which should be inserted inside

Carrying a condom doesn't mean you're desperate for it . . . it just means you're responsible!

BY CHUSITA

INTERESTING FACTS 😮

In history: In ancient Egypt, people were already using contraceptives to cover the penis and hold semen. They were made out of the intestines of goat or fish.

In museums: At the Science Museum in London, you can find a condom from 1798. It's shaped like a phallus, with a pair of loops at the base to hold it in place. It's made from pig's stomach, and it was advisable to soak it in milk before using.

In society: The female contraceptive pill was invented in the 1950s but was not widely used until two decades later, for "moral" reasons! In Europe and America, the pill was first prescribed to help stop menstrual cramps, and in Spain people had to leave the country to buy it!

In art: Nowadays, the use of contraception is so widely accepted that there are even artists who create their own collections—condoms with cool and innovative designs, which look like tattoos when you wear them!

the vagina, up to the entrance of the uterus, stopping semen and other fluids. Both are also safe for practicing anal sex.

Something that you should be aware of is that condoms are **ONE USE ONLY**, no matter how much you wash them! It's also not advisable to use the same condom for two different practices, for example, when changing from oral to vaginal sex, because the material may have been damaged. And you should definitely never use the same condom you have used for anal sex for anything else, because this can spread feces and cause really nasty infections.

One other note: Some people are allergic to latex or some spermicides that are used with condoms. For this reason, condoms are made of different materials and can be made and labeled spermicide-free.

Always carry one!

Whatever your sexual identity, carrying a condom could help you out in a tight spot.

In your wallet or purse, in your backpack or bag . . . it could definitely be worth it someday!

Your condom should be worn correctly. If it's not, it could break. This is more of a risk the first few times you use one, so it's not a bad idea to carry a few extra just in case.

Stand your ground!

If the other person doesn't want to do it with protection, stand your ground. If you insist and tell them it's either with a condom or not at all, they'll probably go along with it. And if they still say no, tell them good-bye, because you're sure to find someone more intelligent and responsible.

Never go unprotected!

There are certain circumstances where it's harder to resist the temptation to go along with unprotected sex. These are risky situations that you should be aware

The advantages of using a condom

- There are lots of different brands and prices.
- They make them for both him and her.
- There are different colors and flavors.
- They're small, discreet, and easy to carry in your purse or wallet.
- They protect against both unwanted pregnancy and STIs.
- You don't need a prescription.
- They're sold in pharmacies, supermarkets, and vending machines.

of, in order to prevent them from happening. In these situations you should be extra careful and be prepared to **DEMAND PROTECTION**. Here are some examples:

- When you have vaginal, oral, or anal sex with someone you don't know very well.

- If you've been drinking, or you feel strongly attracted to someone, or dizzy with lust . . . and all you want is sex!

- If you're a girl and you don't have other contraception.

- When the other person assures you they're clean and there's no need to worry. Or when a guy says he'll control his ejaculation or "pull out" so the girl doesn't get pregnant. It doesn't work like that.

- If you or the other person changes partners often.

- If the other person tries to persuade you to use bogus contraceptive methods (like the ones listed on p. 76).

Contraception for girls ⚲

These are contraceptive methods that don't protect you from STIs; they're just used to prevent pregnancy.

Contraceptive pills: They're taken once a day for 21 days, leaving a week for menstruation in between. They're made of different hormones that stop you from ovulating. It's a simple method that works well for lots of people.

The contraceptive patch: You stick it on your skin and should change it once a week, for 3 weeks out of every month. It works in the same way as the pill, adjusting hormone levels and inhibiting ovulation.

Vaginal ring: It is placed in the upper part of the vagina and lasts for 21 days. You can get it from your doctor or at certain health clinics, and it's easy to use and simple to insert and remove.

The contraceptive injection: Administered by a health professional, it lasts up to 12 weeks.

IUD coil: A device that needs to be placed inside the uterus. It can last between 5 and 10 years.

Diaphragm: A device that is placed inside the vagina between 2 and 6 hours before sex and stops sperm from entering the cervix. It has a few disadvantages, including the wait between inserting it and having sex.

Spermicide and vaginal spermicide: Substances that kill sperm. They're easy to use, although they can cause allergic reactions—and they're best used alongside barrier-based contraception.

⚠ These methods will NOT protect you

There are **TONS OF URBAN MYTHS** going around, saying that certain practices will stop you from getting pregnant.

DON'T BELIEVE THEM. If you trust in any of these stories, you're just as likely to get pregnant as you would be from the missionary position!

You can still get pregnant if:

- It's your first time.
- He pulls out.
- He ejaculates outside the vagina.
- She doesn't have an orgasm.
- She's on her period, it's the day before she starts, or the day after she finishes.
- You do it standing up.
- You're doing it in water.
- She douches after sex.
- She urinates after sex.

Emergencies

The emergency contraceptive pill or **MORNING-AFTER PILL** is not a form of contraception, it's an emergency measure for when something else fails—for example, if a condom breaks or something unexpected happens.

It's definitely not advisable to let yourself get carried away by lust, reassuring yourself that the next day you can just get a pill at the pharmacy. To start with, this attitude leaves you open to contracting STIs. In addition, it's not good to abuse the morning-after pill due to the high levels of hormones it contains and its side effects, which range from tiredness to nausea, headaches, and dizziness. It can even disrupt your period. And let's not forget the price. This is definitely not a standard form of protection. . . .

Unreliable methods

Some people don't worry about STIs, either because they have a partner who they trust or for another reason, so all they want to avoid is pregnancy. This is not a good practice at all.

Similarly, maybe you've heard of natural methods, which rely on avoiding sex on days you are ovulating. **THEY'RE NOT RECOMMENDED** for young women, who can have more irregular cycles. They rely on you knowing your basal temperature, which is your temperature when your body is fully at rest. To measure this temperature you need a basal body thermometer, which is more accurate than a standard one.

Lots of factors can influence your basal body temperature reading, such as broken sleep, drinking alcohol, changing the thermometer . . . and you also need to stick to a strict routine, which is not always an easy thing to do. Basically, this method is just not particularly recommended, because it makes life harder and is unreliable!

FROM ME TO YOU . . . 👍

I have a boyfriend and we use a condom when we have sex, but he wants me to take the pill to make it easier. I've heard the pill has lots of side effects, like weight gain, or even that it can make you infertile. I'm scared . . . what should I do?
M. R., 17

The first thing I'd tell you is to go to your doctor and discuss all your concerns with them. Nowadays, contraceptive pills hardly have any side effects. In any case, it's your body. Don't feel like you have to start taking pills if you don't feel ready, and keep using a condom whenever you have sex.
CHUSITA

MASTURBATION

😄 **Slang**

Masturbate

touch yourself

have some "me time"

self-pleasure   **yank**

Female masturbation

finger yourself

buttering your muffin

beat the beaver

stroke the pussy

Male masturbation

jerk off   wack off

beat the one-eyed monster

blow your wad   **Han Solo**

make the bald man cry

beat off   crank one out

empty the pipes   five finger shuffle

Mutual masturbation

circle jerk   playing chopsticks   **petting**

Finger banging

It can happen suddenly: a touch, a sexy picture, a message, or a slight caress . . . **SOMETHING AWAKENS** in the intimate parts of your body, something you'd never felt before. It's strange, maybe you still don't understand it, or know if it's good or bad . . . but you know you need to explore these new sensations. **DON'T BE AFRAID**.

Privacy will be your best friend. In the bathroom, in your bedroom, in your bed, probably beneath the sheets, when everyone thinks you're asleep . . . You start to touch yourself, finding out what you like and what gives you pleasure, and you'll also find out what you don't like. **YOU HAVE YOUR WHOLE BODY TO PLAY WITH**.

Caress yourself, touch your ears, your throat, your lips, your chest, and breasts—all this will make you aroused and keep you wanting more.

The best way to get to know yourself is to begin **LITTLE BY LITTLE**. It's normal to stop short when you're first starting out, and sometimes you might even just leave it for tomorrow. This is no problem—it's your intimacy and you decide the pace you want to go at. **YOU HAVE ALL THE POWER.**

MYTHS AND MISCONCEPTIONS

CHUSITA tells the truth

"If you masturbate you'll get zits, grow hair on your hands, and go blind."

NOT AT ALL! Although your great-grandma might've been told stuff like this, nowadays we know that masturbating is pleasurable and benefits your health.

"Girls don't masturbate."

WHAT? Girls DO masturbate; maybe they just DON'T go around shouting about it.

"Men get aroused by anything."

NOT JUST MEN! Male arousal is often caused by visual stimulation, and for this reason guys tend to have more opportunities to get turned on, while girls tend to be aroused by their imagination, so it happens a bit more privately.

"Boys masturbate more often (and faster) than girls."

NO . . . There are guys who don't really like masturbating and some girls who love it. And the speed depends on each individual and their pace. If you only think about the climax . . . you're not always going to get there.

"People who don't masturbate are weird."

WHO'S WEIRD? There's no obligation to masturbate. If you don't like it, don't do it, simple as that.

"People masturbate because they don't have a partner; if they did have someone they wouldn't need to."

DEFINITELY NOT! Having a partner doesn't stop you from masturbating, quite the opposite. Often, being in a relationship increases your estrogen or testosterone levels, so if you have a sexual relationship with someone, you can still want more!

In self-exploration, you can use your whole body.

BY CHUSITA

Masturbation is the best way to **GET TO KNOW YOURSELF INTIMATELY**. It allows you access to your most sensitive pleasure points and your own erogenous zones. It helps you know your own sexual tastes. It teaches you about what you like and also about what you don't like. **YOU'RE THE BEST PERSON** to try it with!

It also **PREPARES YOU** for sexual relations in the future, and for great orgasms. The more comfortable you are with yourself, the more you'll enjoy being in a couple and the greater pleasure you'll be able to experience. Also, it will help you enjoy yourself. Masturbation **PUTS YOU IN A GOOD MOOD**, it helps you relax, and it's good for your health and your complexion, along with a whole host of other benefits.

FROM ME TO YOU . . . 👍

For a few months now I've been . . . well . . . masturbating. I don't think it's wrong, and it feels good; the problem is I can't orgasm and it worries me. I spoke to my doctor, who said it was normal for someone my age. I'm scared that my boyfriend will think it's his fault if I don't come, but it's not like that. What can I do?
M. B., 14

An orgasm shouldn't be everything. What's important is that when you masturbate you feel pleasure, and if you do orgasm, even better. But don't be frustrated if you don't get there. You can try different techniques or ways of touching yourself to see how you feel, but do it without stressing yourself out about climaxing. **CHUSITA**

FEMALE  MASTURBATION

First things first: **LET YOUR IMAGINATION RUN WILD**. Imagine a scenario and start to **FANTASIZE**. Sometimes, you might feel ashamed, but if you find yourself with some privacy and you have time . . . don't deny yourself!

Exploring yourself, **PLAYING WITH YOUR BODY,** and seeking pleasure is something natural. You'll start touching above your clothes, feeling how they rub against your body. Sometimes, just a brush over your nipples or crossing your legs can **FEEL GOOD**, whether your underwear's on or not. Some girls use soft toys or pillows, either to imagine they're embracing someone or to rub between their legs.

How does a girl masturbate?

When **YOUR HAND TOUCHES** your most intimate places, it's better to go little by little, noticing what you find along the way. Enjoy your breasts. Play with your nipples. Push down on your pubis with the palm of your hand, stroke the hairs, feel your vulva, open up your outer labia, and stroke your inner labia, then gently touch the clitoris to help it emerge . . .

If you're not wet enough, use your saliva and wet your fingers before continuing.

BY **CHUSITA**

As you start to touch yourself, your vagina will start to get wet. This is a **NATURAL LUBRICANT**, which the body produces when you're aroused and helps make everything easier. If you're not wet enough, you could feel uncomfortable. If this happens, use your saliva and wet your fingers before continuing.

> 🔥 The clitoris is tucked away and moistens and grows when you are aroused. Its only function is to give pleasure. It's so responsive that sometimes it can actually be too sensitive to touch directly. It's best to gently get closer to it, by playing with yourself, massaging and stroking in a way that makes you feel good.

From clitoral to vaginal

Female masturbation includes clitoral and vaginal stimulation. Some girls like one more than the other and some girls like both. Each to their own taste. **IT'S ALL ABOUT EXPERIMENTING** until you find what gives you the most pleasure.

One of the most erotic pleasure points of the female body is the clitoris. Before anything else, you should be aware of the following two things: **IT'S ONLY THERE FOR PLEASURE**, and you should also remember that it's delicate. So you need to approach it calmly and gently.

Another place that's **VERY SENSITIVE** is the rim of the vagina. Stroking it will help you become wet and aids penetration. The usual way to go about it is to first use one finger, either the index or middle, slipping inside with rotating movements.

Find a position that allows you to do this **HOW YOU WANT TO**. Then, if you feel like it, try with more fingers. Don't launch into searching for the mystical G-spot yet, because when you're lost somewhere inside your vagina it's not easy to find. As you get to know yourself, you'll discover that you can stimulate the vagina and the clitoris at the same time. You'll see how sensations change **WITH YOUR POSTURE**: lying down, standing, facedown, sitting, squatting... Enjoy your **DESIRE TO EXPERIMENT**.

Reaching an orgasm ... or not

At the start, having an orgasm might actually scare you. Don't be worried, there's no reason for an orgasm to be the aim of masturbation. The **PLEASURABLE SENSATIONS** that you experience start to increase and get better with practice, and it's normal for an orgasm to surprise you **WHEN YOU LEAST EXPECT IT**. There are some experts who can reach an orgasm in just 4 minutes. There are others who can continue on to have more than one in a row.

 Other benefits of masturbation...

- It relieves tension and anxiety.
- It improves mood and relieves fatigue.
- It lessens menstrual pains.
- It builds your confidence in yourself.
- It helps overcome self-consciousness and other psychological barriers.

MALE MASTURBATION

An advertisement, a suggestive photo, a sex scene in a movie . . . for boys, it's easier to become aroused by **SIGHT**. When you start to masturbate, do it in private and take your time to **FIND WHAT FEELS GOOD**.

Masturbating is not just about relaxing, or something that has to be done as part of a routine. It's best to connect with your arousal, progressing slowly and discovering **YOUR BODY'S DIFFERENT REACTIONS**.

Masturbating helps you find out what you do and don't like, without judgment, and also helps you **PREPARE** for future shared sexual experiences.

How does a guy masturbate?

The penis is not the only player in male masturbation.

Stroking your torso, stimulating your nipples, and, of course, **EXPLORING** your genitals along with **ALL OF YOUR BODY PARTS** will help you feel new sensations. Lubricating lessens friction and stops irritation. You can do this with saliva, or with special products, but be careful because this is a sensitive area.

As you become **AROUSED**, it's natural to gradually get an erection. With your dominant hand you can play with your glans, pulling back the foreskin and gently stroking the body of the penis, holding and massaging it with **MORE OR LESS PRESSURE AND SPEED.**

With the other hand, you can stroke the scrotum, feel your testicles, and explore until you reach the anus, which is also an important pleasure point. Remember that **SENSATIONS CHANGE** depending on your position: standing, sitting, lying down, or in the fetal position . . . **EXPLORE THEM.**

The feeling of penetration

Often what you'll want to experience is what real penetration would feel like. To achieve this sensation, **CONCENTRATE YOUR ENERGY** into the penis, moving the pelvis and keeping your hand still.

Some people try doing this with pillows, although it's not very hygienic. Another option is to use a rolled-up towel, which can be washed afterward, while wearing a condom to stop scraping. Some people also put two sponges together, making a hole in the center. Basically . . . be creative. **YOU DECIDE.**

Orgasms

There's no rush to have an orgasm. When you **COME CLOSE TO CLIMAXING**, changing your speed and breathing deeply will help you delay ejaculation and continue to enjoy the stimulation . . . or you can speed it up to get there quicker.

Putting slight pressure on your testicles after ejaculating can also give you a **PLEASURABLE AND LIBERATING** sensation.

Penis in hand ☞

THE CLASSIC: You hold your penis with all your fingers, with your little finger near the base, and you slide your hand up and down in rhythmic movements.

THE STRANGER: Instead of using the hand you write with, use the opposite one. You'll see that with less technique, it'll feel more like someone else is doing it.

THREE FINGERED: Hold the penis halfway up, with your thumb on one side and your index and ring finger on the other, and start moving back and forth between the base and the foreskin.

WITH THE SHEETS: Cover your penis with a soft sheet, hold it over the cover, and choose whichever technique you prefer from the above.

WITH A CONDOM: You put on a condom and masturbate; the feeling is similar to penetration.

Common methods

MORNING WOOD: A dream turns you on; you wake up hard and make the most of the time before you go out into the world. Charge your batteries for the whole day.

THE CLEAN FIX: In the shower, where the water lubricates and makes rubbing easier. It'll make you feel fresh and healthy.

THE LAZY BOY: When you're home alone, bored and with nothing better to do. 100% guarantee that you'll enjoy yourself.

THE INSOMNIAC: In the middle of the night, when you just can't get to sleep . . . It relaxes you and helps you sleep naturally.

☹ Going limp

If you ejaculate too early, **DON'T DESPAIR**. This can happen the first few times you try, when nerves get in your way. With practice, masturbation can help you **CONTROL WHEN YOU CLIMAX**. You'll be able to delay it, and prolong the experience little by little before ejaculating.

My girlfriend masturbates too much and wants to make love with me less and less. What can I do?
O. F., 17

Talk to her! No one masturbates too much— each person masturbates as much as they need. It might help you two to try out some new things to improve your sex life. So talk to her and ask her.
CHUSITA

OMG!

Exploring yourself, playing with your body, and seeking your own pleasure is natural.

BY
CHUSITA

MUTUAL MASTURBATION

It could happen at a party, when you least expect it, or on a planned date you've been waiting for forever. You kiss **SOMEONE WHO YOU REALLY LIKE**, you hold each other, and you both get carried away with lust, without wanting to go all the way. Welcome to petting, the most common form of **FOREPLAY**.

Don't force anything: if one of you doesn't want to continue, don't do it. It has nothing to do with being frigid. Both of you need to be **CONSENTING AND WILLING**, in a place that, if possible, offers you some privacy and makes you both feel calm. Exploring each other is an **EXTREMELY GRATIFYING ACTIVITY** . . . Enjoy it!

Touching and communicating

The first time you touch someone down there and let them touch you, you have to **BE MORE CONSIDERATE THAN EVER BEFORE**. To start, kisses can go on for as long as you like, and go beyond the mouth, to the neck, to your earlobes . . . The best indicator of mutual desire is when the embrace becomes more intense, and one of you gently **MOVES TOWARD MORE INTIMATE AREAS**. First over your clothes and after, slowly, under them.

Don't just dive in with techniques from the movies. It's not about raising and lowering your hand over and over again, or just sticking your finger in. The best way forward is to **PROGRESS GRADUALLY**, noticing the way your partner reacts and your own feelings, checking if you're enjoying what you're doing. It always helps the experience if you can talk about what you like and what you don't, with **TRUST AND A SENSE OF HUMOR**.

Some techniques

FACE-TO-FACE: Watch how your partner masturbates, and at the same time, show them how you do it. It's a great way to become aroused and **RID YOURSELF OF EMBARRASSMENT**.

TAKE TURNS: Concentrate on giving your partner pleasure, and enjoying it, and then switch. It's a very sensual experience, which helps you get to **KNOW EACH OTHER**.

AT THE SAME TIME: Touching and being touched at the same time **INTENSIFIES SENSATIONS** and your understanding of each other. A word of caution to beginners! Although you might be getting hotter, remember that your partner might be going at a different speed, so don't forget to check how they're doing.

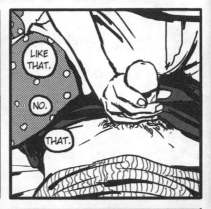

Rules

- Wash your hands!
- Check that you're lubricated enough. If you need a little extra help, you can use saliva or even scented lubricants.
- Enjoy each other, without setting goals.
- End the game if you're not enjoying it.
- Enjoy your mutual understanding!

A body of another sex

When you explore a new body that's different from your own, you don't know how it feels . . . **NO ONE IS BORN KNOWING**! It's best to be able to discover it gradually, exploring penises, vulvas, testicles, vaginas, and anuses, and experience how different things feel. When you are touching, the important thing is that both of you enjoy it.

A body of the same sex

Here, you can try to do **WHAT YOU LIKE BEST** when you touch your own body, with your partner, although this is not guaranteed to work out. There's no perfect way to masturbate: what one person likes might irritate someone else. It's best to be very considerate, asking and sharing.

The most important thing is to notice the other person's responses, to see if you should keep going . . . or try something else!

BY
CHUSITA

Pleasuring a girl ⚲

Putting your hand down a girl's pants to explore requires delicacy. Do it gently, avoiding harsh movements wherever you touch her. Stroke her outer labia, which will make her clitoris erect. This pleasure point is very sensitive to touch, and also very delicate. Give it the attention it deserves.

The rim of the vagina is also very sensitive. Stroking it will help a girl to become wet, with a natural lubricant that stops her from being hurt when you slip your finger inside. **GAUGE HER REACTIONS**, asking her how she feels, and stop if it seems like she's not enjoying it. If she likes it, you can try using more fingers, or even your other hand to explore further.

Pleasuring a boy ♂

Putting your hand down a guy's pants and exploring the bulge tucked between his legs takes a certain bravery. He might not be aroused enough, and you'll find his penis is flaccid. Or you might find it's already very stimulated. Stroke it with an open hand, gently touch his testicles and fondle them . . . Little by little, you may see how **HIS PENIS HARDENS**.

Lubricating your hand can help you massage his penis more easily. It's normal to start by stroking the tip (the glans) and pulling the foreskin back (the skin that covers it), if he has one.

Then, you can close your fingers around it and start **SOFTLY MOVING** them up and down, speeding up as his arousal increases. You can also gently stroke his testicles and, if he likes it, you can use your other hand to explore further.

Orgasm?

Enjoying the excitement of being touched with your hands, next to someone you like a lot, is definitely worth trying—and if you manage to reach an orgasm, even better! However, **THIS IS NOT ALWAYS POSSIBLE TO ACHIEVE**. In a couple, it might be that neither of you gets there, that only one of you does, or that both of you manage it, at the same time or separately. There are lots of different ways!

Sometimes you might experience a mental block and, no matter how aroused you are, you aren't able to climax. There are girls who end up being irritated and boys who can't become erect. Sometimes, the foreplay goes perfectly, but you still aren't able to orgasm, or you come too soon.

You have to deal with this patiently, calmly, and with a sense of humor. If it doesn't happen now, it'll happen later. **WITHOUT FORCING ANYTHING.** It's simply a question of experiencing and getting to know each other bit by bit.

LET'S...

GET TO KNOW EACH OTHER

When you're attracted to someone, you enter into a **WHOLE NEW WORLD**! From desire and the playful first stages to first kisses; from first getting intimate to when you fully explore each other's bodies for the first time. Being with someone you like and who likes you back is its own reward, because you can have some really great times together.

Relationships ... or not?

There's no point in putting a label on your relationship in order to **GET PHYSICAL**. Two people can do a lot together without any strings attached if they don't want them. There's also no pressure to have sex ... or to get married, for that matter!

Sometimes you get intimate with someone because you're curious or **YOU WANT TO TRY IT**. Sometimes it's because two people are attracted to each other. Occasionally, all these feelings coincide: the right mind-set, **DESIRE**, and newfound **EMOTIONS** that blossom within both of you and are expressed outwardly, just like that.

Online?

Social media helps you connect with people easily, which is amazing—**SOMETIMES**. You can look at photos of the person you like, find out who their friends are, what they are in to ... But don't scrutinize someone's profile, because this could come back to bite you later. We don't always present ourselves in the same way online as we do in real life. So it's much better to have the other person reveal their character and tastes to you themselves!

The internet is a perfect place to communicate, send messages, and flirt with someone, although keep an eye out because **IT CAN ALSO BE VERY DANGEROUS**. If you start a conversation with somebody online and begin sending them compromising pictures or messages, it's like placing intimate parts of yourself in someone else's hands. However much you trust someone, you'll never know who could get access to your device, or who might see what you've sent or who you are actually talking to. You also can't be sure, once your relationship is over, whether your private correspondences will be made public on social media!

MYTHS AND MISCONCEPTIONS
CHUSITA tells the truth

"To fool around with someone, you first have to act dumb."

YOU MIGHT, but you don't have to! If you fool around with somebody and use your brain at the same time, you can often still get what you want!

"Kissing with tongues is dirty."

IT DEPENDS! It's not nice to stick your tongue down someone's throat or kiss someone when you've got bad breath . . . But a passionate French kiss will send tingles down your spine! It's just an exchange of saliva.

"If you let someone touch you 'down there' you might as well go all the way."

STOP RIGHT THERE! Just because you let someone touch you once, because you wanted it then, that doesn't mean you can't slam on the brakes if you change your mind later. You set your own limits and your partner needs to respect them.

"If you're with someone you can't fool around with anyone else."

YEAH, YEAH. That all depends on the agreement you have with your partner—and on your own desires, which can change and appear when you least expect them to! Even when you're completely head over heels for someone, you might experience the desire to mess around with someone else from time to time. Whether you act on these impulses or not should depend on what you have **AGREED UPON WITH YOUR PARTNER**. It is always important to consider each other's feelings.

Be careful when trying to define a relationship; you might find the longer you think about it, the more you both want to take a break.

— BY —
CHUSITA

QUIZ

ARE YOU TWO FEELING THE HEAT?

Your partner really turns you on, and it seems like you get the same reaction from them . . . But are you two feeling the heat? Complete this quiz and add the numbers up to get your temperature reading!

When you see them . . .
1° You're happy and go over to them.
2° You go crazy with the desire to kiss them.
3° You throw yourself on top of them and won't let go for anything.

When they see you . . .
1° They're happy and come over to you.
2° They go crazy and try to kiss you.
3° They throw themselves on top of you and won't let go for anything.

When they're with you they're . . .
1° Shy and take things slowly.
2° Forward, but not over the top.
3° Romantic and always looking for a good opportunity to make out.

When you're with them you're . . .
1° Shy and take things slowly.
2° Forward, but not over the top.

3° Romantic and always looking for a good opportunity to make out.

Since you've been going out . . .
1° You've gotten to know each other a bit more.
2° You're getting along great!
3° You can't stop kissing!

When you kiss . . .
1° It's only ever a peck.
2° Your kisses are romantic.
3° It's always a passionate make out sesh.

When you say good-bye . . .
1° You say you'll call soon.
2° You set a date for next time.
3° You text five minutes later, saying how much you miss each other already.

RESULTS

(Between 7° and 10°) ❄
Taking it slow
Things seem friendly, but maybe it's time for you to express yourselves!

(Between 11° and 14°)
Clear attraction!
You're obviously attracted to each other . . . but who's going to make the first move? If you want this to go any farther, someone needs to take the initiative!

(Between 15° and 18°)
Hot stuff!
You love to flirt and get turned on by the slightest thing. Lots of kisses, plenty of fun . . . You leave wanting more!

(Between 19° and 21°)
You're on fire!
You're clearly very into each other and you never miss an opportunity to get it on. What are you waiting for?

DESIRE ☺

Desire is a sensation that arises naturally and **YOU DON'T GET TO DECIDE WHEN IT HAPPENS**. It happens, simple as that. You like someone and you want something to happen, whether it's to kiss, start a relationship . . . or whatever! You have to control your desire, at least until you find out how the other person feels.

You can decide not to tell someone you have feelings for them, although the passion will start to tear you apart from the inside! It's best if one or both of you decide to show it . . . at least a little! **SELF-CONTROL** is necessary for a number of reasons: first, so you don't scare the other person, and second, so you don't do anything **YOU'LL REGRET LATER**.

😮 Did you know . . . ?

In the movie *Raiders of the Lost Ark*, the main character, Professor Indiana Jones, gives lectures in a room full of students with crushes on him. One of them actually tries to get his attention by writing "LOVE YOU" on her eyelids. But all she manages to do is make him nervous!

The object of desire

It is one thing to desire another person and another to **LUST AFTER THEM**. When you experience lust, you might be momentarily attracted to someone. It could be someone you've never thought about in that way before. It's not the person who's made you feel this way, it's just that a feeling of lust has come over you. There's nothing bad about it, but you should be aware that it can happen to you . . . and that it could also happen to someone else, toward you.

And remember that desire doesn't necessarily mean love: you can desire someone very intensely without falling in love. Although, sometimes desire is the first stage of a longer, more intense relationship.

Reciprocated?

All things, especially the good ones, take **TIME**. Remember that each person experiences a relationship at different levels of intensity. It's good to listen to yourself, and listen to the other person. And when the time comes . . . read the chapter about fooling around!

You know they want you when . . . 👉

- They make eye contact when they talk to you.
- They try to catch your eye.
- They lick their lips.
- They smile flirtatiously.
- They unconsciously stroke their cheek, hair, or beard.

Not reciprocated . . .

When you desire someone who doesn't feel the same way, it's normal to feel frustrated. However, you always **GET OVER IT IN THE END**. Don't torture yourself, or convince yourself that no one will ever feel the same way about you, because this doesn't help and it's not true.

If, on the other hand, someone lets you know that *they* desire *you* but you don't feel the same way . . . You should **MAKE THIS CLEAR** right from the start! You can't force yourself to feel something you don't, and you don't want to lead them on. It's best to show how you feel, as kindly as possible — even if it disappoints them. Think about how you would want to be told.

You may have a crush on someone **UNATTAINABLE**—like a teacher, a mentor, or someone older than you in a position of authority. This is **INAPPROPRIATE**.

Don't become obsessed and, most important, **BE VERY CAREFUL**. Don't come on to them, because you could end up making a fool of yourself and regretting it. Even if you get a positive response, this type of relationship will probably not end in a beautiful romance, because imbalances, caused by age gaps or differences in sexual maturity, mean both parties can end up dissatisfied. Channel your desire elsewhere and look for someone else.

FROM ME TO YOU . . . 👍

I'm crazy for the lead singer of my favorite band. I spend all day thinking about him, I download every photo of him I can find online and I can't stop looking at them. I follow all his social media profiles to see what he's doing . . . Am I in love with a celebrity? **P. L., 15**

Maybe! But for it to be real, he would have to know you exist. I'm sure you'll soon fall in love with someone who can love you back! **CHUSITA**

FOOL AROUND

When two of you both desire each other, you can start to fool around! Fooling around, **FLIRTING, SEDUCTION, MAKING OUT**...you can give it a hundred different names, but the desired result is always the same: to get into bed with the person you like!

These early moments should be savored **PATIENTLY**, because although they can feel like a long time, in reality they're usually very brief. During this stage, you walk around all day with a smile on your face, you can't get the other person out of your head, and it's clear you're also in their thoughts.

WHAT A HIGH!

This playful stage is a very fun part of a relationship, and it often begins with **LOTS OF LAUGHS** and leads to...the first kiss! It's important to laugh together as this really helps you to bond—and to talk, of course. Don't miss a single opportunity to communicate and get to know each other better.

When you're fooling around with someone, you end up **FANTASIZING MUCH MORE**. The more you hang

INTERESTING FACTS

In history: Ladies used to woo their suitors...with fans! There were a series of coded messages to signal that they would accept a date, or wanted more!

In photography: One of the most famous kisses in history is an image of a sailor and a nurse. Their photograph was taken in 1945 during the celebrations of the end of World War II and was published in *Life* magazine.

In literature: A number of authors have written about the fictional character Don Juan, who was able to seduce every woman he met.

In film: The musical *Grease* follows the story of a couple who have a summer fling. When the vacation ends, they think they'll never see each other again, but they soon realize they go to the same school...and have to win each other's hearts all over again!

In the animal kingdom: The males of some birds, such as the peacock, have flamboyant plumage that they use to attract females. Birds of paradise sing and perform a courtship dance as well as show off their plumage.

out and the more your wishes become reality, the more you will fantasize.

But watch out, **DON'T GET TOO CARRIED AWAY**! Have realistic expectations, so you don't end up demanding too much and getting disappointed.

In "flirting" mode

You like each other, traded numbers, you're friends on social media, you leave each other cute comments, and fill each other's timelines with emojis . . . This is how courting works in the 21st century! It's an exciting, addictive game, but don't let it go on forever. While you're laughing together, using smileys and exchanging cute gifs, you should also be thinking about the right moment to move on to **SHARED** smiles that happen **TOGETHER** and **IN PERSON**. Meet up, whether it's at school, at the park, or wherever you normally see each other. Or you can arrange a traditional date: grab a coffee, go to the movies, or do anything, really. This is the next stage, and it's **VITAL** if you want to go farther and start kissing.

Signs they're flirting

- They wink at you.
- They blink a lot when they're looking at you.
- They send you romantic emojis.
- They laugh a lot while you talk.
- They brush against you suggestively.

Negative signs

- They don't listen to you.
- They don't reply to your messages.
- They cross their arms when they talk to you.
- They avoid you and slink away from you whenever they can.

KISS 😚

When your desire is reciprocated, the first kisses soon follow. I'm talking long, meaningful kisses, not quick pecks that are stolen as part of a game like truth or dare. You have to really **TASTE** a first kiss. And it has to be wanted by both parties.

Even if you've never kissed anyone before in your life, you don't necessarily need to go looking for how-to videos online or do the old practice session with your own arm. Kissing is something we all know how to do instinctively and **THERE'S NO NEED TO BE SCARED** of doing it wrong. As soon as your lips make contact with someone else's, you'll know how to proceed. You don't need an instruction manual. This is also something that improves with practice!

You might encounter a few teething problems the first few times you try kissing, or a situation might make you feel inexperienced. If you bump teeth, or there's too much saliva, if you accidentally bite your partner, or if you both start going at different rhythms—**LAUGH IT OFF** and carry on! There's no need to be embarrassed by it because things will smooth out soon enough.

We're kissing!

During your first kisses, which tend to be more hesitant, it's normal to **CLOSE YOUR EYES.** It allows you to feel the contact more deeply, the sensation of lips on lips, the pressure . . . When you kiss, it's not only your lips that connect. When your face is that close to someone else's, you'll notice their breathing, their heart beating . . .

At certain points you might be tempted to **OPEN YOUR EYES**, to look at the other person's face. It's fine to try it a few times, to check if they're enjoying it, but don't do it just to spy on them! It's best to let things take their course, **ENJOY EACH MOMENT**, and see the positive in whatever happens.

FROM ME TO YOU . . . 👍

Hi, I've got braces and the girl I like does, too. Will they get in the way if we kiss?
J. M. S., 14

No, not at all, you just have to be careful not to end up getting caught on the braces and stuck together. Although if you really like this girl, you'll probably want to stay stuck to her! **CHUSITA**

Basic preparations

- Freshen your breath. Brush your teeth or chew mint gum.
- Wet or moisten your lips if they're dry.
- Throw away your gum before kissing. It could be unpleasant.
- Drink water so you don't have a dry throat.

- Don't wear too much lipstick.
- If you're a guy, shave your beard, because it could irritate your partner's skin.
- Don't open your mouth too wide, or go straight in with the tongue.

KISS AGAIN

After the ice is broken with the first kiss, there's no end to the games you can play with your mouths. As your passion grows, your kisses will change and **THE TONGUE** will come into play. You could start by softly touching the tips, and slowly turn it into a full French kiss.

A work of art!

Kissing with tongue isn't particularly complicated, but like everything . . . it takes practice! To have a **GOOD KISS**, there are some things you shouldn't do. Don't shove your tongue straight into someone's mouth or let it flop there like a piece of fish, and don't stick it down their throat and suffocate them.

Types of kisses

STOLEN: A kiss that happens by surprise, when one of you is caught off guard. It could be the start of something more intense . . . or lead to a telling-off!

PECK: Brief touching of lips. Also known as a "graze." A classic among friends and relationships that are just starting out.

LITTLE KISSES: A succession of small kisses. Lingering, more sweet and romantic.

WET: Mouth to mouth, lips slightly apart, and heads tilted in opposite directions. Very, very seductive.

SMOOCH: Mouth to mouth, with more pressure, turning from side to side. Also

called the "Hollywood kiss" because it's very showy.

VAMPIRE KISS: One of you sucks the other's lip. It's very sexy, but don't overdo it—it might cut off circulation!

FRENCH KISS: Kissing with tongues moving together and giving it everything, playing a game of back and forth between two mouths.

TONSIL HOCKEY: A kiss that goes so deep that it touches your uvula. Not everyone enjoys this . . .

THE EXPLORER: A kiss that happens somewhere else on your body.

French kissing is all about finding the other tongue and turning it into a game, because it's best when both tongues—and people—are involved. It's not about moving your tongues around like washing machines. The tongue is full of nerve endings, and lightly touching it is **HIGHLY PLEASURABLE**. Ah, and don't forget to breathe, or you could get dizzy!

More often and better!

As soon as you've gotten the hang of it, you'll find that there are **THOUSANDS OF WAYS TO KISS**. Every kiss is different and there's a world of possibilities. By changing the intensity, speed, or depth of your kiss, you'll broaden your horizons!

Beyond the mouth

When you kiss your partner, you don't just have to use your mouth! Kisses on the nose, for example, can be very playful and romantic. Kisses in other places can be very sensual, such as on your eyelids, although you should be very gentle with them. It's also fun to nibble softly on your partner's earlobes. And there's the neck, where you can play with your tongue and your whole mouth, increasing arousal.

☺ Some advice

Sucking the skin too hard can create a mark called a hickey. Don't give someone a hickey without asking them first. It's not fun to have a mark on your neck that reveals what you do in private.

TOUCH 👉

When you kiss your partner passionately, it's kind of implied that you will touch each other! Bodies brush against each other and you're sometimes not sure what to do with your hands. **HUGGING AND CARESSING** your partner not only heightens the quality of your kiss, it also opens you up to new sensations. Touch is one of the most pleasure-enhancing senses and it allows you to **GIVE AND RECEIVE** pleasure at the same time.

In principle, it's best not to jump right in; let cuddles and caresses come about naturally. Touching someone's hair, neck, or hips . . . It's something that happens spontaneously and usually gets you wanting to **EXPLORE FURTHER**.

You have to be cautious about where you touch your partner, making sure not to invade their privacy or expose your own.

Touching each other with your clothes on doesn't mean you have to go any farther if it's not the right time.

BY
CHUSITA

Sometimes you can touch your partner **OVER THEIR CLOTHES**, knowing that that's as far as it will go. In other, more intimate moments, you'll test out new ground and see where things take you. It's best to begin with your tops on, making sure your partner is comfortable and that they are happy for you to touch them. Exploring with your hands also **REQUIRES PRACTICE**!

Touching a girl

Stroking a girl's hair will allow her to **RELAX AND ENJOY HERSELF**. The neck and shoulders are also very sensitive areas and stroking or softly massaging them with your fingers can be enjoyable.

However much you want to **FEEL HER BOOBS**, don't start there! Explore her back, her waist, her hips, her thighs . . . and then begin to move up, slowly, starting from her navel upward, gently, and noting her responses. If she seems uncomfortable, stop. And if she tells you to stop, stop.

Breasts are an **EXTREMELY SENSITIVE** part of a girl's body. In situations like these, they tend to get firmer; her nipples will become erect. If both of you want it, you can stroke her breasts gently, first with the tip of one finger and then with more, even using your whole hand or both hands. Then, if things progress, you can try touching her crotch over her pants.

Touching a boy

Boys are generally very sensitive in the nape of their neck, and holding it or stroking it can make them feel **SECURE**. You could, for example, massage this part of his body with an open palm, using the tips of your fingers, and then reach up into his hair and scalp. If he's wearing any jewelry or has piercings, play with them, as you're sure to find them in sensitive places. But don't go overboard, or these areas could become irritated. Whether they're muscular or not, the shoulder blades and upper arms tend to accumulate tension and stroking them will **RELAX AND AROUSE** him.

However much you want to **TOUCH HIS CROTCH**, don't start there! Explore along his spine, his hips, his butt, his thighs . . . and then start to slowly move toward his front, gently reaching into his pockets or the front of his pants. If he seems uncomfortable, stop. If he tells you to stop, stop.

The penis is an **EXTREMELY SENSITIVE** body part. In situations like these, it tends to increase in size and become hard, and it can cause him some discomfort under his clothes. Caress it gently, first with an open hand and then with your fingers, moving up and down around the fly of his pants. Everything depends on how far you two want to go.

WHERE HAVE YOU BEEN HIDING? I MISSED YOU.

HA-HA. BUT WE JUST SAW EACH OTHER AN HOUR AGO IN MATH!

AH, EVERYONE CAN SEE US...

TOUCH AGAIN

Touching your partner is another, **MUCH MORE SENSUAL** form of intimacy. As you start to get to know each other from above... you'll also want to get to know each other down below. Classic **HEAVY PETTING**!

When you start to enter this new level of intimacy, don't rush, or you might end up pressuring your partner. The chemistry between you two will determine the pace and the way you proceed.

Initiating

Finding the right moment to touch your partner is not always easy. Going **UNDER THEIR CLOTHES** takes tact! Don't skip the initial stages: kiss first, touch them over their clothes, and then find the right moment to go farther, with the other person's permission!

If you notice that your partner isn't enjoying what you're doing, **STOP**. Take your time! It's good to notice each other's responses in shared intimacy.

A good way of going about this is to show your partner that you want **THEM TO TOUCH YOU**, whether it's on your breast, your butt, your vulva, or your testicles. Maybe they're scared! Give them time. And if they do it, enjoy the feeling!

Touching a girl again

Once you've touched her breasts above her clothes... you'll be dying to get under them! **TEST THE WATERS** gently. Caress her breasts first with an open hand, enjoying their size and shape. Do this carefully and gently, because they can get irritated.

Before putting your hand down her skirt or pants, make sure she's aroused and willing. And **DON'T EVEN THINK ABOUT** sticking your finger straight into her vagina! Find your way carefully, touch her vulva, and check her responses before going farther. And read the chapter on masturbation!

☺ Some advice

Don't act like a FAIRY-TALE PRINCESS, expecting everything to be done to you. And don't turn into a CAVEMAN who's just out for his own pleasure. You should enjoy the other person and help them enjoy you.

Touching a boy again

However much you've touched his crotch over his pants, it's best to start going under his clothes by touching his **UPPER BODY** first. Place your hand under his shirt, touch his chest, stroke his pecs, and stimulate his nipples, which are very sensitive. And then go down and start to explore under his pants.

If he's only a little turned on, you'll need to be gentle and stimulate him, to increase his arousal. On the other hand, if his penis is completely hardened and erect, try touching him again. Stroke his glans and explore the body of his penis. And read the chapter on masturbation!

Create situations that arouse both you and your partner, because true pleasure happens when you're both enjoying it.

GET NAKED

Once the physical contact between you and your partner has intensified, and if it's the right time and place, you might want to show each other **YOUR NAKED BODIES**. It's natural to feel shy or embarrassed—everyone feels like this, especially the first few times. If you've gotten to this point, it's because you like each other, just as you are.

It can happen in a number of ways. When they get more used to it, partners usually **UNDRESS** together, taking off each other's clothes. At different times, especially the first few times you undress with someone, it's easiest when each person undresses themselves, because it stops you getting tangled up in clothes. One of you might have more experience than the other and take charge of the situation, undressing themselves and then helping the other.

Every situation requires a different approach: let yourself be guided by what you want and what feels most comfortable. Bear in mind that the end result is always the same: **TWO NAKED BODIES**.

Rules

- Don't be embarrassed or make excuses for your body.
- Don't judge your partner or ask questions about their appearance.
- Don't turn it into a competition of who's more in shape.
- Show your body naturally.
- Admire your partner's body and make them feel comfortable.

FROM ME TO YOU ...

I'm embarrassed to let my boyfriend see me naked, and although we touch each other a lot under our clothes, I never get fully naked. What should I do? **M. J. R., 16**

What you need to do is to start feeling comfortable in your own body. Prepare yourself: undress alone and in front of the mirror, take in all your good features, and shout out loud how great you look. This will boost your confidence and self-esteem. Also, remember that the fact you have gotten to this point with your boyfriend is because he really likes you, and thinks you look just fine, too. He wants to see you and be with you. I'm sure you're pretty excited to see him naked, too. **CHUSITA**

Just like the movies?

Advertising, movies, and other forms of media often show the "idealized" naked body, both male and female, generating unrealistic fantasies. Not every body is long, lean, and muscular—nor should it be!

Before beginning, know one thing: **THERE IS NO SUCH THING AS PERFECTION!** Rid yourself of preconceived images and misconceptions, because this is the only way to put your complexes and insecurities aside, for you and your partner.

In your underwear

Seeing someone in their underwear is **SEXY**. It doesn't necessarily matter what kind it is either; plain cotton underpants could be enough. In any case, you get to decide what you do. Go down to your underwear only if you feel comfortable. Also, don't feel pressured to take it off with the rest of your clothes.

Striptease?

When you are first getting to know your partner intimately and getting naked for the first time, it's best to **FORGET THE SHOWBIZ** and leave stripteases for the movies. Unless you're well practiced, or you do it with a sense of humor, a striptease could feel ridiculous and cause the exact opposite of the desired effect. In my opinion there's nothing less erotic than someone taking off their socks **WHILE HOPPING**!

Leave fears about your naked body behind and try to feel comfortable, because then you'll be able to really enjoy being in a couple.

😮 Did you know . . . ?

One of the most admired stripteases happened more than twenty years ago! It was performed by Kim Basinger in the film *9½ Weeks*, and her dance, along with the song that played, is now used for most stripteases.

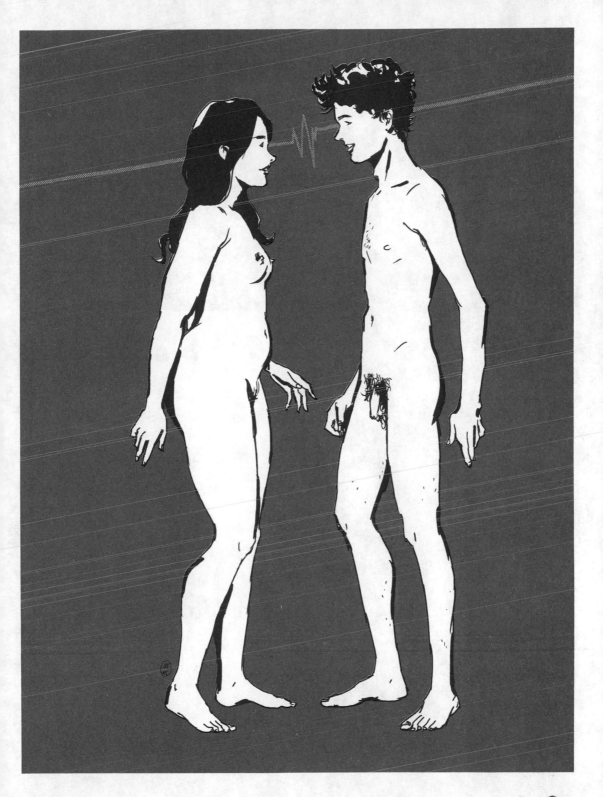

HOOKING UP

The day will come when you decide to have sex for the first time, and sex will start to be a part of your life. This is a **PERSONAL DECISION**, which you need to make responsibly, calmly, and, most important, on your terms.

You could plan it in advance . . . or just let it happen! Whatever you do, **DON'T FORCE ANYTHING**—especially the first time.

Expectations

No one would deny that the first time you have sex is an **IMPORTANT LIFE EXPERIENCE**. However, there are a lot of misconceptions surrounding your first time that you shouldn't believe. Some people say it should be amazing, that you'll feel fireworks, that you'll be in heaven . . . **DON'T KID YOURSELF**, because in the majority of cases it doesn't go like this. Just like anything you try for the first time, the first time you have "real" sex, lots of things will go wrong and it won't be what you expect.

To start with, **NERVES TEND TO GET THE BETTER OF YOU** the first time. It's normal to be affected by your nerves, but don't be overcome by them, because they'll stop you from enjoying it. Don't overthink things, worrying if you're doing it well, whether you look good or not, if the other person is judging you . . . Try to relax and lose yourself in your body, concentrating on your own feelings. Enjoy it.

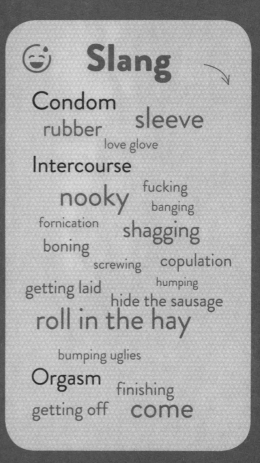

😄 **Slang**

Condom
rubber   sleeve
        love glove
Intercourse
    nooky   fucking
            banging
fornication   shagging
boning
        screwing   copulation
getting laid   humping
        hide the sausage
roll in the hay

        bumping uglies
Orgasm   finishing
getting off   come

MYTHS AND MISCONCEPTIONS

CHUSITA tells the truth

"If a girl doesn't bleed the first time she has sex, it means she's not a virgin."

UH, NO. Sometimes the hymen has already broken from something else unrelated to sex. Anyway, it's the 21st century for goodness' sake; this is not something to be disappointed or pleased about.

"Sex with a condom isn't as good."

LET'S NOT KID OURSELVES: IT'S DIFFERENT, but you need to put yourself and your health before anything else so you don't end up with a nasty surprise. Always think about protection first. And sex with a condom is fun, too!

"Having lots of sex stretches your vagina."

NOOOO! The vagina doesn't widen with sexual activity. It's quite the opposite actually, because sex makes your muscles work harder and strengthens them. Widening of the vagina happens for other reasons, for example while giving birth.

"The only way you can orgasm is with penetration."

LOL NO. Both he and she can have an orgasm if the clitoris, penis, or anus is stimulated. You can reach an orgasm through masturbation and oral sex, too.

"When you have sex you have to moan loudly."

IN MOVIES PERHAPS! Moaning—or not moaning—should come about naturally, although normally you won't raise your voice much when you and your partner are living with other people . . . Anyhow, people should express themselves however they like.

"A guy can never refuse when a girl offers sex."

FALSE. Very, very false. A boy can say no to sex if he wants, in the same way a girl can say no if she doesn't feel like it. Either one can refuse. Sex must be consensual.

If you have sex with someone, both of you should enjoy it. It's not good to be selfish!!

BY CHUSITA

ARE YOU READY FOR YOUR FIRST TIME?

Sometimes you want it . . . sometimes you don't! You think you'd like it, but at the same time you're scared. Do you really want to do it? Complete this quiz, add up the results, and find out!

You think about it . . .
- If you're honest, hardly ever.
- • Sometimes, when you feel desire.
- • All the time, you can't avoid it!

How much do you know about sexuality?
- Not a lot. You're up for finding out more.
- • You know what it's about but you're still unsure.
- • Lots. You've read about it and you know your stuff.

You define yourself as . . .
- Insecure, you often doubt yourself.
- • You let yourself get carried away by your emotions.
- • You are in control of your impulses and you know what you want.

Relationship-wise, you . . .
- Don't have a partner, and don't like anyone in particular.
- • There's someone you like a lot, but you haven't really started anything yet.
- • You have a partner . . . and can't wait to get intimate with them!

You are led by . . .
- Your head; you overthink everything.
- • Your intuition; it never fails.
- • Your heart; anything is possible!

You get hot if . . .
- Something really special happens; otherwise, barely ever.
- • You're kissed or touched by the person you like.
- • You're with the person you like, or fantasizing about them!

After a romantic encounter . . .
- You feel happy and want to do it again.
- • You can't stop thinking about the other person.
- • You're so turned on you need to find some privacy to really let loose.

RESULTS

(Between 7 and 10 •)
Not at all!
Whether you're lacking confidence—or just aren't that interested—don't feel pressured to jump into anything. Give yourself time; there's no rush!

(Between 11 and 14 •)
You're of two minds
Sometimes you feel like this could be the moment, other times you're not so sure. Don't get too worked up about it! When the right time comes, you'll know what to do.

(Between 15 and 18 •)
Diving in head first!
You want to do it, but you still haven't found the right person . . . Hopefully they'll turn up soon!

(Between 19 and 21 •)
You're a love machine!
You're filled with desire and you know who you want . . . The only question is when! The "how" will be figured out.

Foreplay

Having sex isn't just about penetration/insertion—it's lots of other stuff, too! It's about seducing your partner and being seduced with kisses and foreplay, too. This will help you gain intimacy and maintain your desire.

Games and foreplay are important between two people, especially the first few times you have sex together. As well as increasing your enjoyment, these initial shared touches will relax you, help you connect, keep you in the moment, and make you want to be even closer to each other!

Often there's no need for penetration, especially when you're not prepared for more or when you have limited time. In situations like this, oral sex or mutual masturbation can be just as satisfying, or even more so.

Start by kissing, as tenderly and sensually as you like.

Then use your hands. The skin is the largest organ in the human body. Why not stimulate it with touch?

Look at your partner intensely and use tender words, or talk dirty.

How do you feel about erotic games? If you want to know more, jump to the section titled "Fantasies and Sex Toys."

☞ Do it if . . .

- You trust the other person and they make you feel relaxed.
- You've tested the waters with your partner and both of you want to do it.
- You've read up on and chosen forms of protection and contraception.
- You've found an appropriate place that makes you both feel comfortable.
- You have time to experiment . . .

☟ Don't do it if . . .

- You're only doing it to make them like you.
- You don't want to but you feel pressured by the other person.
- You don't have a condom or another form of contraception.
- The place you've chosen isn't private enough.
- You hardly have any time to experiment.

False expectations

You've probably seen a lot of **SEX SCENES** in movies and on TV shows. But remember that actual sex isn't an onscreen fantasy. Girls aren't lingerie models and boys aren't muscled Adonises. In the same way, sex doesn't just happen with two people's eyes meeting across a crowded room and them falling straight into bed, consumed with lust.

Don't fall for the hype! Sex isn't so wild and frenzied. Really, especially at the beginning, it's **THE COMPLETE OPPOSITE**. Don't force anything. The more naturally both of you act, the more comfortable you'll be together. When it comes to positions, they tend to happen by themselves as you become more passionate. And it's better to go calmly than quickly!

In a pair

Sex between two people is about making it pleasurable for both of you and **CONTRIBUTING EQUALLY**. Girls aren't passive objects and guys don't dominate heterosexual intercourse, and in any relationship, you don't need to adopt dominant and subordinate roles of outdated sexist traditions! Each of us can be more passive and sensitive in certain situations, and more assertive or seductive in others. When we're in a relationship we support each other just as we are.

Don't sweat over . . .

UNDERWEAR: In the real world, neither boys nor girls care about it as much as you think. If you want to, keep it on, and if not, take it off. Whatever you wear, be sure it works for you!

BODIES: The body you have is yours, and if you've gotten this far with your partner, they probably think it's incredible. Be comfortable in your own skin, explore what your body can do, and move with it as well as you know how.

HAIR: It's not obligatory, or even necessary, to remove hair from any part of your body. Some people, both boys and girls, feel good when they shave and others don't care.

Don't forget . . .

TO STAY CLEAN: Everything about you should be clean, especially your intimate areas. Getting clean could also be a good chance to shower together, if you can, because this increases arousal.

MULTIPLE CONDOMS: Make sure you have extras, especially when you're not very experienced. No matter how many times you've read the instructions or how many video tutorials you've watched, you still might put it on wrong. You learn with practice.

LUBRICANT: It's better to have it for more comfortable intercourse. But if you don't have it, you can always use saliva, and lots of it!

Get practicing!

At the start, it's best **NOT** to set yourself crazy goals, or assume that sex should always end in penetration. There are many ways to experience sexuality as a couple, and **EVERY ENCOUNTER** is different. It's better for each of you to set your limits, so you know how far you're prepared to go and what you'd like to try. You can enjoy playing around without unrealistic expectations, starting with masturbation and advancing little by little.

Maybe you both enjoy masturbation, and when you have intercourse, you don't enjoy it as much. Don't think of sex as a race, either, and don't feel like you have to compare yourself with others, wishing you could get to where they are and feeling left behind. It's not a competition!

☺ Did you know...?

The Kama Sutra was written in India between 400 and 200 BC, and it's believed to be the first sex manual in the world. It is one of the most influential books in world history, and includes very detailed instructions about different sexual positions.

Remember, no matter how far down the line you are, if you don't want to continue, don't. **YOU CAN ALWAYS SAY NO.** Then, depending on how you feel, you might want to backtrack a bit and keep enjoying each other, or maybe just leave it for another time.

ORAL SEX 😜

Stimulating your partner's genitals with your mouth—tasting the most intimate parts of them, and letting them taste yours—is highly pleasurable! This is one of the most arousing ways to **HAVE FUN** with your partner. It can be your entire sexual experience, form part of foreplay, or be used after intercourse to reach an orgasm.

Different names for different practices

During oral sex, your lips and tongue come into contact with your partner's most intimate parts. Doing this with a penis is called **FELLATIO**, and with a vagina it's **CUNNILINGUS**. In addition, there is a third sexual activity that is generally known as **RIMMING**, and this involves stimulating the anus.

> **Don't practice oral sex if . . .** ⚠️
> - You don't trust your partner and you don't have a form of contraception.
> - You can see warts or marks on your partner's penis or vagina.
> - You have oral herpes or an open sore on your mouth.

As usual, it's always best to start with touch, to arouse and stimulate your partner's intimate places before going in with your mouth. The first few times you should **ADVANCE SLOWLY** so you can get used to this new technique naturally. It's not about quickly shoving your penis into someone's mouth. It's about making contact and getting to know a new way of having sex.

You shouldn't feel bad about enjoying fellatio or cunnilingus. It's normal! Actually, you can gain **A LOT OF ENJOYMENT** by watching your partner enjoy themselves as much as you, or even more, as well as from the act itself. It's absolutely normal to want your partner to do the same to you—get into it and see where your pleasure takes you.

Do you enjoy practicing oral sex? Congratulations! Go for it and remember, you learn by practicing.

BY CHUSITA

Basic hygiene

Although you might have showered in the morning, it's not a bad idea to go to the bathroom and wash your intimate parts and your pubic hair before oral sex. By doing this, you'll get rid of any bad smells and freshen up your skin.

If you have very long pubic hair and you think it could get in the way, you can trim it a little to make it less of a problem. In any case, get used to the idea that during oral sex, a hair might get in your mouth. Don't stress about it!

Communication

Even though the definition of the term *oral sex* has nothing to do with speeches or elocution, **YOU CAN STILL TALK**! Nowadays there are no taboos about it, and communicating with your partner can really improve your sex life. It's very important to say what you want them to do to you or what to avoid, and it's also important to listen to what your partner wants you to do and how you should do it. This will help you enjoy things more and give your partner more pleasure.

FROM ME TO YOU ...

I've been going out with my boyfriend for a while and I'm embarrassed to let him go down on me. I'm scared of him putting his head down there, but I do want to try it. What would you do?
P. T., 18

How to perform cunnilingus

Before going straight for the vagina, caress her **BREASTS AND NIPPLES**, stroke her stomach, her belly button, and the area between her legs, gently, waiting for the clitoris to poke out. When you can feel that she's aroused, kiss her thighs and explore her outer labia. Be careful with your teeth: you can bite her a little on her legs, but not any further. When you go into her vulva, cover your teeth with your lips so you don't irritate her. Use **YOUR FINGERS** to help you, opening the outer labia and sensing for the clitoris with the tip of your tongue. It's very sensitive, so **PLAY WITH IT** gently, but when it's aroused it grows, and it can be kissed or licked with more intensity. Whatever you do, don't overstimulate the clitoris, as it can be become irritated and unpleasant.

You can also move lower, down to the vagina itself. **SLIDE YOUR TONGUE** around the rim and insert it slowly inside, using your fingers to help you. The more you moisten this area with your saliva, the more pleasurable it will be for the both of you.

Don't try to simulate penetration with your fingers or with your tongue. Keep a steady rhythm: not too light, not too fast.

You might not like it, but you won't know if you don't try. You'll probably have to start with some other things first, regular masturbation for example, and let him slowly get closer to your vagina and play with it. Relax, try to enjoy the moment, and see if you really do like it or not. **CHUSITA**

How to perform fellatio

Hold the base of the penis with one hand and put your mouth **ON THE GLANS**, or the tip of the penis. This is where he'll feel the most pleasure. You can have fun playing with the glans, kissing or licking it with the tip of your tongue in small movements. When you put the penis into your mouth, be careful with your teeth— it's important not to scrape him with them. Move your head gently, letting the penis slide in and out slowly. Use your tongue to play with the glans and apply pressure with **YOUR LIPS**, to simulate penetration. As you do this, you can stimulate the base of the penis with your hand. You can also move your hand to stroke his testicles.

Put the penis as far into your mouth as you feel comfortable. Don't go deeper than you want to, because it could make you feel sick. Then, **VARY YOUR RHYTHM**, increasing the speed as your pleasure is heightened.

> ## Never . . .
>
> - Go straight to it and do it mechanically.
> - Make a disgusted face when you're giving oral sex.
> - Compare their penis or vagina with previous partners'.
> - Give or receive oral sex when you don't enjoy it.
> - Ejaculate with no warning.

When practicing oral sex, your safety comes first!

Always use protection

Unprotected oral sex carries the risk of contracting sexually transmitted infections. So if you're not in a stable, monogamous relationship, and you're not completely sure that you and your partner are completely clear of STIs, it's best to do it with a **CONDOM** or **DENTAL DAM**.

A condom is the best form of protection for **FELLATIO**. Most are made of latex and have a faint rubbery flavor. You can rub saliva onto the condom with your fingers so you don't notice this. Or you could use a flavored condom—there are lots to choose from! Another, more imaginative option is to use flavored lube.

To practice **CUNNILINGUS**, you also need to use protection, and a dental dam is best for this. If you want to get rid of the taste of latex, you can apply some flavored lubricant on one side.

For **RIMMING**, you use the same type of protection that you would for cunnilingus, so either a dental dam or a modified condom. It's important to lubricate the anus well before placing the latex over it, as this area can easily become irritated. You can find more information about lubricants in the "Anal Sex" section.

Sperm and vaginal fluid

Even when you're in a stable, trusting relationship, and you decide not to use a condom, that doesn't mean you have to enjoy the taste of sexual fluids! You can decide whether to **SWALLOW** or not, depending on what you enjoy, and not because your partner wants you to, or you feel pressured to.

However you decide to do it, you shouldn't experience any negative side effects after swallowing your partner's vaginal fluid or sperm, providing your partner is healthy and free of **STIs**. Some people love to **FILL THEIR MOUTHS** with their partner's bodily fluid; others prefer to spit it out or use it as a cream to massage another part of their body. Do what you like, as long as it is your choice.

Giving . . .

Practicing fellatio or cunnilingus is not just about giving pleasure to your partner. Don't forget to enjoy yourself, too. Only do it when you **BOTH WANT TO**.

When you're exploring new parts of your partner's body with your tongue, it's good to **PAY ATTENTION TO THEIR RE-SPONSES**. See if they're enjoying it, and find out what gives them pleasure. If what you're doing is not getting the desired re-

sponse, don't force it. Find a new posture, move to another area, or change your rhythm and technique. And when you do find their most sensitive places and the best way to stimulate them, make the most of it.

There's no reason to focus exclusively on your partner's genitals when you're giving oral sex. **USE YOUR HANDS** to stroke their buttocks, their stomach, their chest . . . You can even stop for a moment to kiss your partner on the lips before continuing.

Receiving . . .

When you are on the receiving end of oral sex, you might be worried. What should you do with your hands? And the rest of your body? Should you say anything or is it best to stay completely silent? As with other types of sex, **THERE ARE NO RULES** for this. However, there are a few tips which will help you to enjoy it more.

To start, relax, find a **COMFORTABLE POSITION**, breathe deeply, and let yourself go. If you like, you can place your hands behind your head and keep them there. Stay there quietly and enjoy your partner's movements. Or, if you prefer, you can touch yourself, or touch your partner. **DO THIS GENTLY**, though, without pushing or forcing them a certain way.

CONCENTRATE AND ENJOY YOURSELF. If something is irritating you, say so, and if you like something a lot and want more of it . . . say that, too! It'll really help your partner. So . . .

DON'T HOLD BACK!

And the finish line?

Let there be no doubt: you can probably **REACH AN ORGASM** through oral sex. Many girls actually find it easier to orgasm through oral sex than through vaginal sex. Some people even say that these orgasms are more intense. Boys can also often reach orgasm through fellatio. However, you might not always want to get there.

Basic positions

LYING DOWN: This is the most comfortable position for both fellatio and cunnilingus. The receiving partner lies down, legs slightly apart, straight or knees bent. The partner who's giving can also lie facedown, or be on their knees in front.

STANDING: The receiving partner stands up, legs slightly apart, and the other partner kneels in front. It's a highly satisfying position for fellatio, because the testicles can be stimulated, although it's more difficult for cunnilingus.

SITTING: The receiving partner sits, with their buttocks apart, legs spread, and back against the chair and the other partner kneels in front. It's a very satisfying position for both fellatio and cunnilingus.

This is especially the case when oral sex is just a part of foreplay and you want to do other things and move on to intercourse. If you feel like you're on the cusp but you don't want to climax just yet, let your partner know. Then they can slow down, touch you more gently, and hold off your orgasm.

In any case, if you're about to orgasm, **WARN YOUR PARTNER**. And, after having a break . . . you can always try again!

69

To give and receive oral sex **SIMUL-TANEOUSLY**, you both need to be facing each other, with your bodies positioned in opposite directions. This is known as 69ing. It's a very mutually satisfying practice, but it's also a very complicated one. For this reason, it's not recommended to do it during the first few times you and your partner try oral sex.

Often, usually when **YOU DON'T HAVE MUCH EXPERIENCE**, 69ing doesn't allow you to focus on both giving and receiving pleasure, and it can cause you both to lose concentration. However, as you get more experienced, you'll know each other better and you'll know what you and your partner like best. Then it can become the most satisfying practice of all.

☺ Did you know . . . ?

Fellatio has actually been depicted in Egyptian mythology! The king Osiris was murdered and cut into pieces by his brother, Set, who then threw the fourteen pieces of his body into the Nile. Osiris's wife, Isis, who had magical powers, managed to find all the pieces, except one: the penis. She made a new one out of clay, placed it onto Osiris's body, and stimulated it orally. She gave life to her husband's body using fellatio.

VAGINAL SEX

At a certain point, you'll feel the need to move beyond foreplay and have sexual intercourse.

Even if you both really want to **HAVE PENETRATIVE SEX**, don't rush into it. Foreplay helps you become aroused and get into the right frame of mind. As you stimulate your pleasure points, you'll start preparing both the vagina and the penis. If you're not aroused, penetration won't be as pleasurable and you might even want to stop.

Erections

If your penis is not **COMPLETELY ERECT**, however much you try to force it, penetration might not work. This can also cause more anxiety and make you lose your erection. Foreplay, masturbation, or oral sex will help your erection become more intense, and harder.

Lubrication

As the vagina is stimulated, it will lubricate itself naturally. The more lubricated it is, the **MORE PLEASURABLE** sex will be. Some girls produce less natural moisture and that's normal. Just use some artifical lubricant to make things easier.

The first time

When you start practicing vaginal sex, you might worry that **IT'LL HURT**. It is true that sometimes penetration can cause discomfort, although it normally doesn't hurt. If you're a boy, discomfort happens when you haven't used enough lubricant, or when your glans or the skin of your penis becomes irritated. And if you're a girl, discomfort can also happen without enough lubricant, or when your hymen breaks and this part of your body dilates for the first time. But all of this can be overcome with **PATIENCE, GENTLENESS, AND THE DESIRE TO CONTINUE**.

Putting on a condom

You need a new condom for each new activity. If you've just had oral sex using a condom, you should put on a new one before penetrative sex, even if you haven't

---

:) **Some advice**

Don't try to put the Kama Sutra into practice when you're just starting. To begin with, find a simple position that's comfortable for both of you. Later you can experiment with more positions!

ejaculated, as sometimes condoms can be damaged by friction. Before penetration, a condom should be placed on your erect penis. Sometimes doing this causes a guy to lose his erection, but anticipation, seduction, strokes, and touching of your intimate parts will often solve all this.

Now!

When you are both ready and the penis is erect and the vagina is moist (and after choosing a form of protection), you can **START PENETRATION**. It's not about charging in or going at it for dear life. No matter how much you want it, you should enter gradually, gently, **WITHOUT RUSHING** and without trying to go too fast. It's important to make sure that neither of you becomes uncomfortable.

Don't forget to stimulate other parts of the body, like the lips. When penetration is accompanied with kisses and caresses, the experience will be far more intense. Try to **FEEL EVERY MOMENT** and enjoy every small movement. Above all else, don't try to reach orgasm as soon as possible, because the journey is more important.

Effort and energy

Going slowly and gently doesn't mean being quiet, hardly moving, and making minimal effort. It's not about twisting around like a contortionist, either.

You should move enthusiastically and **RHYTHMICALLY**. It's best to share the effort, meaning that you don't end up with one of you putting in lots of energy while the other barely moves. Instead, you should try to keep the same rhythm. Some people say that making love is like dancing, and as the dance progresses, the partners become more coordinated. It's all a matter of practice.

Talking . . .

Heavy breathing and panting aren't the only sounds you can make! Although in principle, saying anything might seem ridiculous, when sexual intercourse begins everything changes! **WHISPERING INTO YOUR PARTNER'S EAR** and having them whisper into yours is extremely exciting!

Remember: it's about being arousing, not having a conversation!

BY CHUSITA

Tell your partner what you like, or say what you'd like them to do—and the more explicit your language is, the more it will stimulate them. You can also ask if they like what you're doing or if they'd like to do something else in particular.

If you didn't love this person before you had sex, don't say you love them now. You should bear in mind that sex can cause confusing feelings. So it's best to **HOLD BACK ON EXPRESSIONS OF LOVE** if you don't feel them in your heart of hearts, and be responsible for what you say. This means you won't end up playing with your partner's feelings . . . or taking them by surprise!

Some people like to hear **DIRTY WORDS**. This is something to start doing little by little and not go into the first few times you have sex, because it can cause the opposite of the desired effect. If you and your partner both enjoy it, it's normal to ask for it. And if it doesn't come naturally, don't do it.

The best phrases

I really like this . . .

That feels amazing!

I'm so excited!

Keep doing that . . .

You're so great!

Yes, I love it!

More, I want more . . .

Watching . . .

You can have sex in the dark, but remember that it's highly arousing to be able to watch your partner enjoying themselves . . . and **LOOK INTO THEIR EYES**! Sight is one of the best senses for sharing emotions. Maintaining eye contact while giving pleasure to another person helps bring out the sexiest version of ourselves.

FROM ME TO YOU . . .

I'm going out with a boy and we both want to do it, but we know we're too young and our friends say we're making a mistake. What would you do? **L. P., 13**

Your friends shouldn't be the ones deciding when you should make love for the first time—it's an important decision that you two should make together. Advice is good, but you need to decide. If you really want to do it, and you feel prepared for sex, alongside everything that goes with it, be responsible, be aware of the protection you need, and try it. But don't feel pressured into it, either—sex is something that should happen naturally. You'll know when you want to do it and when your time has come. **CHUSITA**

We increase **DESIRE** by using our eyes and through shared gazes. This nonverbal communication can be very useful for sharing emotions that we can't express with words. It can show the affection we are feeling, how much (or how little) we like what we're doing, how much we're enjoying ourselves . . . All of this makes us feel more secure and raises our self-esteem.

Missionaries and Amazonians

When you're just getting started, it's best to stick to **BASIC POSITIONS**. Just because they're basic doesn't mean they're boring. Quite the opposite! If they've been able to bring pleasure to millions of partners for centuries, you should really consider them!

Of all the positions, the most well-known and commonly used is **MISSIONARY**, where the guy is on top of the girl. It's comfortable, easy to do, and allows the penis to penetrate the vagina properly and get up to the G-spot. It's a good position for kisses and caresses and allows you to look each other in the eyes, if you want to. Don't think that just because he is on top, he's the only one who should guide your movements, because you can both move your pelvis rhythmically, heightening pleasure.

Never . . .

- Talk about your or your partner's flaws.
- Talk about exes or compare your partner with others.
- Take a selfie during intercourse.
- Stop to answer the phone.
- Take this chance to talk about stuff that's on your mind.
- Call your partner by another name.
- Insult your partner or confuse dirty words with derogatory language.

The version of the missionary when the girl is on top is called the **AMAZON**, another of the most well-used basic positions. This not only allows you to gaze into each other's eyes, it also makes gazes even more intense, as it creates distance between your bodies. Here, it's the girl who is placed on top of the guy, in a half-sitting position over his pelvis, guiding the initial penetration. After this, both bodies can move with the same rhythm, making this position highly pleasurable for both partners.

Further variations

Both the Amazon and the missionary positions have variations that can really **IMPROVE YOUR RHYTHM**. Here are some tips:

- Whether you're on top or underneath, close your legs while contracting your pelvis. You'll feel more pressure on your genitals and they'll be even more stimulated—you and your partner will notice this.

- If you're in shape, you can tilt your pelvis, while arching your back, and make a small inward and outward movement. You'll experience an intense feeling of friction!

- If you're underneath, bend your knees and wrap your legs around your partner's waist above you. The penetration will be even deeper.

- If the person underneath raises their legs up toward their shoulders, their partner on top will get more thrust and this will make the penetration more intense.

As you practice, you'll find your own natural positions. Dare to be creative!

BY **CHUSITA**

Other positions

THE TOTEM POLE: The boy stands up and the girl wraps her arms and legs around him, hanging from his body as he penetrates her. He needs to be strong enough to hold her. If you get the balance right, this is a very pleasurable position!

THE LAPTOP: One of the couple sits on the bed, a chair, or a steady surface. The other partner sits on their lap and guides penetration. It has two variants: you can do it face-to-face, or if she's on top, back-to-front!

THE BICYCLE: Standing, she gently leans forward, resting her hands on a wall, and her partner penetrates her vagina from behind. It's an adventurous and sensual position that allows for deep and intense penetration.

THE LOTUS FLOWER: Both of you are sitting on the bed or a steady surface, facing each other. Cross your legs together in an intimate embrace that brings your genitals together. It is one of the deepest and most intimate sex positions, as it brings your chests together and makes it easy to kiss.

THE PYTHON: Begin penetration in the standard missionary or Amazon position. Then straighten out your bodies completely, one on top of the other, keeping your legs close together. Both bodies will come completely into contact and place intense pressure on your genitals, generating lots of pleasure!

How long does it last?

The length of penetration varies. It could be very short, lasting only a couple of minutes. Alternatively, it could go on for up to 30 minutes! The average duration, according to some studies, is around 7 minutes, and ideally between 7 and 13 minutes. However, there's no need to time yourself or get worked up about the duration, because the most important thing is to enjoy yourself. Take all the time you need, relax, and try to be sure you're both satisfied by the end of it.

You don't need to be a contortionist to have good sex. There's a position for every body!

BY **CHUSITA**

Announcing your orgasm

An **ACCUMULATION OF SENSATIONS** will let you know you're starting to climax and coming to an orgasm. Letting your partner know when this happens, by using a simple phrase, such as "I'm getting there" or "I'm ready," will prepare them to share this moment with you and respond to your anticipation.

Simultaneous orgasms, when both of you come at the same time, can be amazing. However, it's actually very complicated, especially at the start of a relationship, so try not to see it as a goal. And don't worry if it doesn't happen: prioritize your pleasure together, and allow each other to **GO AT YOUR OWN PACE**.

Delaying orgasm

If you feel like you're about to come, or that your partner is, you can **PROLONG YOUR PLEASURE**, if you want to. Don't be embarrassed about stating it explicitly, because it will feel good for both of you. If you stop for a moment and stay still for just twenty or thirty seconds, your bodies will maintain the energy to go a little longer before reaching orgasm. However, like always, this is all about practice. At the start, you won't be able avoid an orgasm, even when staying still. Delayed orgasm is

ADVANCED-LEVEL STUFF!

😎

How does girl-on-girl sex work?

There's more to girl-on-girl sex than masturbation and oral sex; contact between genitals can also play a big part. And penetration (with your fingers or with a sex toy) is not always essential! It's common to start by **RUBBING YOUR THIGHS** against your partner's genitals, and vice versa. Then lie facing each other so you can touch clitorises.

Mutual penetration with your fingers or specialized sex toys is an added pleasure! Your fingers can be used to penetrate with a variety of movements and even varying girths, allowing for a whole host of different sensations. Many of the aforementioned positions work with two girls. Some require the use of a dildo for penetration for one of you, or by using a sex toy that allows both of you to experience vaginal pleasure at the same time. (Find out more in "Fantasies and Sex Toys" on p. 148.)

The **SCISSORING** position allows both of you to experience more intimate and intense genital contact. Sit facing each other, lean back, and rest on your hands or elbows. Weave your legs together so you can rub your genitals between them.

The first movements are usually quite gentle, as you lightly press your vaginas together and try to get both clitorises to touch. From there, you can try to vary the position. It's all a question of practice, imagination, and desire!

When one of you doesn't get there . . .

If only one of you has an orgasm, don't feel like all you can do is give up and feel unsatisfied. Not at all! **YOU CAN CONTINUE** in a number of ways and try to get both of you to climax.

In heterosexual sex, when **THE GIRL** climaxes first, it's generally not a problem to continue penetration, and the guy can go on. However, sometimes the vagina contracts after an orgasm and it becomes painful to have the penis inside.

When **THE GUY** climaxes first, he usually loses his erection after ejaculation, as well as the stamina to keep penetrating until the girl comes.

In both cases, or for non-heterosexual sex, you can make the most of your arousal and continue to give pleasure to your partner through masturbation or oral sex. Don't be selfish, and remember that orgasming isn't always the goal.

FROM ME TO YOU . . . 👍

Since I started having sex with my boyfriend almost a year ago, I haven't had a single orgasm. It bothers me, because I'd really like to have one. What can I do?
A. M., 18

First things first—don't get yourself worked up! Sex isn't just a physical experience, it's a mental one, too, and that also goes for orgasms. On the one hand, you have to be in a certain frame of mind, and on the other, you need to know yourself. Try exploring yourself, finding your most sensitive pleasure points, and when you know what they are, tell him to stimulate them. You might also want to try new things, experimenting with new positions and techniques while you make love. And if he reaches an orgasm and you don't, he can continue with oral sex to try to get you to orgasm, too.
CHUSITA

Afterward

When an encounter comes to an end, you should **DEAL WITH IT CALMLY**. It's not acceptable to finish and rush to leave, each person going their own way; this tends to be pretty disappointing. You can't expect your partner to be very energetic, either, or suggest big activities to do together. But it also isn't good to just shut your mouth and say nothing. Take your time! Caress, kiss, talk, relax, and continue making each other feel good, even if you do have to say good-bye.

What next?

After a pleasurable session, you'll obviously be feeling good. There's no need to feel remorse or worry about how well it went—quite the opposite. Remember **JUST HOW MUCH YOU ENJOYED** this time with your partner and be happy about it. If something in particular didn't go well, or now, after having some space, you think you could have done better, **MAKE NOTE OF IT**! Next time make improvements.

Alternatively, if something made you feel bad, and instead of feeling satisfied you're at rock bottom, go through the possible reasons. If it's because you don't feel good about your partner, or you felt forced into things you didn't want to do, **DISTANCE YOURSELF**. Remember that the person you owe the most loyalty to in the world is yourself. The only real love that you'll always have, the person you should care for above all else, is you.

Again and again . . .

When a relationship develops between two people, and sexual encounters happen naturally, the sex tends to **IMPROVE AND BECOME ENRICHED**. Don't be scared to experiment. If both you and your partner like it, why not give it a try? There's a world of sexual activities that go beyond vaginal sex; there are also techniques and sex toys that help enrich the sex life of any couple. Don't miss out on them!

It's best not to 😠

GO STRAIGHT TO SLEEP: Okay, you used a lot of your energy, but don't go to sleep without at least telling your partner how much fun you had!

ABSENTMINDEDLY CHECK YOUR PHONE: This is definitely impolite—in addition, if you do this straight after sex, it gives the impression that you haven't enjoyed what you were just doing. Any contact with the outside world can wait five or ten minutes more.

RUSH OUT: Although you might be late or in a hurry, take five minutes to enjoy this postcoital bliss, and make sure your partner is okay. Then, say good-bye kindly.

ANAL SEX

Anal sex is a **NORMAL ACTIVITY** for all kinds of people, regardless of their sexual orientation. Both men and women can enjoy practicing it. The only thing that's essential is for both of you to be sure that anal sex is something you'd like to do.

The anus is full of nerve endings, which makes it one of the **MOST EROGENOUS** parts of the body. Stimulating it while well lubricated is one of the most arousing activities you can do, and it opens up a universe of new sensations.

Out with taboos!

Many **HETEROSEXUAL** guys are scared about wanting to be penetrated anally. There's no reason to be afraid or worried. Wanting to enjoy your body by experimenting with anal sex is not at all

Anal sex is something that we can all experiment with and make one of our most pleasurable experiences.

negative, and it doesn't have to make you doubt your own sexuality. You just like to experiment! Girls can give anal sex to their male partners, if both of them feel like it.

Rigorous hygiene

Before practicing anal sex, it's important to clean this area **VERY WELL**. Plenty of water and soap are essential. You should also very carefully clean your **FINGERS AND NAILS**, and make sure they're as short as possible and that nails are filed down, in order to avoid scratches and cuts.

Enemas

Odor and fecal matter can be an unavoidable result of anal sex. Always wash thoroughly afterward, and **DON'T GET EMBARRASSED**, this is normal. If it's a frequent problem, the receiving partner can give themselves an enema beforehand—but only use warm tap water. You can buy disposable douches at most drugstores, or reusable ones where sex toys are sold. (Thoroughly wash reusable douches between every use.) Don't overuse enemas; keep them to once or twice a week, and experiment to find out what works best with your body.

Extreme caution

Although anal sex carries no risk of unwanted pregnancy, it's one of the most dangerous practices for contracting sexually transmitted infections, as the anus accumulates lots of bacteria. It's also a very sensitive area in which it's very easy to open up small wounds. You need to be cautious and always use a condom.

To use lubricant or not to use lubricant?

Unlike the vagina, the anus has no form of natural lubricant, which means it resists penetration. So lubricant is essential if you want to practice anal sex in a **HEALTHY AND PLEASURABLE** way.

Saliva is a good lubricant for your intimate areas; however, for anal sex, saliva is not enough. The most convenient thing to do is buy **SPECIALIZED LUBRICANTS**, sold in drugstores and specialty shops, which help moisten and soften the area.

The best lubricants for all sexual practices are **WATER-BASED**. They don't damage condoms, unlike oil-based lubricants. It's important to make sure they don't contain Vaseline, as this can cause infections. Among the wide range of lubricants on offer, you'll usually be able to find one that's specifically designed for anal sex; it's normally denser. It's easy to use: apply a few drops to the anus, and another few to the tip of the penis (over the condom). Some are more refreshing and others aromatic, to heighten pleasurable sensations.

Preparing the anus

The application of lubricant can become a **SENSUAL MASSAGE**, which helps the anus to dilate and makes penetration easier. Stimulating the area with your fingers will help keep the first moments from being painful. It's good to massage in circular motions around the anus and slowly and gently introduce the fingers. When you do enter with the penis, do it carefully and slowly. This means that both of you can enjoy the moment 100%.

FROM ME TO YOU ... 👍

I've been with my boyfriend for six months, and at the beginning he wanted to be the active one in our relationship, and was happy with me being passive. Recently, he asked to change around, with me penetrating. I tried, but my penis didn't work and I couldn't get an erection. What should I do? **L. M. S., 18**

Remember that in every relationship, both partners should be generous. And if something went wrong once, because of nerves or surprise and the newness of it, it doesn't mean it will always be that way. Try practicing on your own, imagining how good this new activity will be for you, too. Then try to put the best parts of those fantasies into practice. If you're still not aroused or you feel like you really don't want to do it, be direct with your partner about it. Oral sex, masturbation, and special sex toys can help you deal with your lack of erection. **CHUSITA**

How does boy-on-boy sex work?

When there are two boys, they tend to establish roles between themselves. Some guys prefer to be **PASSIVE**, letting their partner penetrate. The other option is to be **ACTIVE**, penetrating the partner's anus. However, you can also be **FLEXIBLE**, taking turns to try both roles and sexual practices.

In order to really know which role you prefer, you have to have **TRIED EVERYTHING** first. When you do put it into practice, listen to yourself and find out what it is you want to do more. It's normal to talk with your partner and agree which role each of you will take.

There should be **AROUSAL AND AN ERECTION** on both sides. The active partner can stimulate the passive partner's penis as he penetrates from behind, increasing the amount of stimulation. If he can't quite reach, the passive partner can masturbate while the partner concentrates on anal penetration.

You can climax together or separately. Just be sure to enjoy it.

😆😅 More Positions

SPOONING: Stretch out on the bed, lying on your side with your legs slightly bent. The receiving partner lies in front, with their back to the other partner, who penetrates from behind. Both bodies mold into each other, making this a very sweet embrace.

THE ELEPHANT: The receiving partner lies facedown on the bed, or on a steady surface, and lifts their pelvis for their partner above to penetrate. It allows for deep penetration and lets both partners control the movement.

DOGGY STYLE: This is a very common position that works well for both vaginal and anal sex. The receiving partner goes on all fours, resting their hands on the bed or the floor, and keeps their back straight. The other partner penetrates from behind, holding their partner by the hips. Highly pleasurable!

THE ROCKING HORSE: The partner who's penetrating lies on the bed faceup with their legs open, arching their pelvis slightly. The other partner sits on top, facing their partner but leaning back slightly. It allows the receiving partner to control movement a bit better, making the experience even more pleasurable!

THE COWBOY: The partner who's penetrating lies stretched out on the bed faceup, with their legs together. The other is on top, back to their partner, leaning slightly over their legs. It allows the one who's receiving to ride their partner's penis, hence the name!

THE MAGIC MOUNTAIN: The receiving partner kneels down over a stack of pillows. The penetrating partner comes in from behind. This also allows you to get to your partner's genitals with your hands!

Boy on girl

For a girl to orgasm from anal sex, you need to also stimulate **THE CLITORIS**. Depending on the position you use, it might be hard for the boy to do this, or he might not be able to reach the area with his hands. In this case, the girl will need to stimulate herself, while her partner concentrates on anal penetration.

Girl on boy

Fingers can easily replace the penis for anal penetration. Enter first with **THE TIP OF YOUR INDEX FINGER** and then, as the anus dilates, use another finger, which will increase girth and depth, making rhythmic, gentle movements.

If you don't want to use your bare fingers, you can cover them with **A CONDOM**, which will help prevent the mucous membrane coming into contact with feces and bacteria. As well as lubricating the anus and the condom, you can also lubricate your fingers using your own saliva, so you can feel the moisture underneath the latex as you explore your partner's body.

☺ Did you know . . . ?

Ancient Greek men practiced anal sex with each other so often that there is evidence of it on decorative urns.

Other precautions

- If you have painted nails, it's better not to insert them into the anus. Nail polish can introduce toxic substances to the mucous membrane.

- Always try to find a comfortable position for both you and your partner. If one of you feels unstable or forces a posture, it could be painful or cause tears in the anus.

- If you want to practice oral or vaginal sex after anal sex, you must go to the bathroom first and wash both your hands and genitals well.

- You should never use the same condom for anal and vaginal or oral sex. A new condom should be used for every sexual activity.

- If you have hemorrhoids, wounds in the rectum, or problems with your colon, it's best not to practice anal sex before consulting a doctor. Make sure you are healthy first, and then enjoy it to the max!

What next?

After anal sex, an activity in which partners sometimes aren't facing each other, it's good to make visual contact and confirm your **MUTUAL SATISFACTION**. One of you might have reached orgasm, or both of you might have. Or perhaps neither of you was able to climax, and you want to continue . . .

DON'T DEPRIVE YOURSELVES!

FANTASIES AND SEX TOYS

Everybody has sexual fantasies, whether we're single or we have a partner. And we don't always share them! This is **NATURAL** and a fundamental part of being human, as fantasies allow us to imagine ourselves in unusual situations.

Having fantasies doesn't always mean we have to put them into practice. Most of the time a fantasy is a **PRIVATE GAME**, which allows us to visualize something that we would never do in real life! Sexual fantasies feed into desire and arouse us even more. And there's no need to keep them private because, if we trust our partner, sharing our fantasies with them can be incredible!

Some fantasies are impossible to re-create and are highly arousing for precisely that reason! Others, however, can be put into practice, as long as both you and your partner want to. These can become some of the most pleasurable activities, which will **REALLY ENRICH** your sexual encounters.

Sexual fantasies increase sexual desire and arouse you even more. And sharing them with your partner can be incredible!

BY CHUSITA

Common fantasies

Imagining . . .

...that someone is watching you having sex.

...that your partner is actually one of your celebrity idols, or a complete stranger.

...that you're having a threesome.

...that you're with a person of the same sex if you identify as straight, or of a different gender if you identify as gay.

...that you're a sex machine, with as much experience as a porn star.

Dildos

In sex shops you can find a **VARIETY OF DIFFERENT DILDOS**. There's a dildo for every type of pleasure imaginable! Among the most basic models, dildos look similar to penises and come in a range of sizes and shapes. You can find one for every sexual practice; for example, some dildos are specifically designed to stimulate the clitoris and the vagina simultaneously, or designed with anal sex in mind. Many girls also enjoy using vibrators for more stimulation of the clitoris.

Every dildo, no matter the material it's made of, should be used **WITH A CONDOM** to protect the mucous membrane from possible infections. And if you change orifices, you also need to change condoms.

You should carefully and thoroughly clean dildos before and after each session, following the instructions that came with them. Some sex toys can be ruined if cleaned incorrectly or with the wrong type of cleaner. And never use a dirty dildo or sex toy!

Improvised toys

Although sex shops are full of all kinds of sex toys, there are also ways to engage in sensual activities with your partner that don't cost money. Many everyday items can help you enjoy highly erotic and pleasurable experiences with your partner. Here are some examples:

- **A FEATHER.** Perfect for tickling your partner's body, even in the most intimate places!

- **A HANDKERCHIEF.** It can be used in lots of ways, to cover your eyes, to tie your wrists . . . What more could you want?

- **A SCARF.** The longer the better. It will let you tie your bodies together. The one holding the ends gets to call the shots!

- **A PAINTBRUSH.** It's a very sensual way of tickling your partner and massaging their body, and it can even be used to paint sexy words on your partner's body. Careful with the paint though! If it's not edible, best to try this with chocolate sauce instead.

- **A BELT.** Ideal for seduction, for holding your partner, dancing sensually . . . or even tying your-selves together.

INTERESTING FACTS 😮

In history: The Egyptian pharaoh Cleopatra is believed to have invented the vibrator, by filling a hollow gourd with bees, which vibrated as they flew around inside!

In medicine: The first vibrator of the modern age emerged during the late 19th century in Britain. It was a device shaped like a penis that had an electric current running through it and was used to "cure female hysteria!"

In the animal kingdom: The males of some spiders tie females up with their thread as they mate; the females, who don't resist, free themselves later, after the act! Also, female praying mantises eat their male lovers during mating!

☝ Remember . . .

Livening up your sexual experiences with music you both enjoy can really increase your arousal! Music makes your bodies move even more, and helps you move together rhythmically.

Erotic games

With a bit of imagination, you can create highly seductive games. Here are some ideas:

- **USE A DIE.** On a sheet, think up two lists with six points each: one list has verbs (*caress, lick, kiss, suck . . .*) and the second has pleasure points (*mouth, ears, navel, buttocks . . .*). You then throw the die twice: the first roll tells you what to do, and the second roll is where you do it.

- **USE CARDS.** You can play strip poker, where you undress each time you lose. Alternatively, you could play with a reduced deck, taking out the picture cards, and assign a sexual activity to each suit (for example, masturbation for diamonds, oral sex for clubs . . .). The number on the card determines how many minutes you have to do it for.

Exciting places

You can find loads of places where sex with your partner becomes a **NEW EXPERIENCE**, all without leaving the house. For example, doing it on a table, on the kitchen floor, or even on top of the washing machine, to enjoy the vibrations!

One of the most well-known places is **THE BATHTUB**, although this doesn't always end up being that pleasant, because water can dry out the vagina or make the penis flaccid. If that happens to you, reduce the amount of water!

Risky activities

If you trust your partner and you both want to try more extreme activities, why not give it a chance? It can be very enjoyable to play with handcuffs and scarves, tying each other to the bed and dominating each other, as long as you establish what you're going to do first. **AGREEMENT IS ESSENTIAL**, to know how far each of you wants to go, and what you want to try.

In a couple, you can try plenty of different things. However, with people you don't know well or when you're not exactly sure what kind of friendship you have with someone, think carefully! Certain games can make you **VULNERABLE** and put you in situations that are hard to get out of. Be wary of group situations, because they have the potential to become awkward. In any case, if you do something, make sure it's because you've thought about it properly in advance and you're totally convinced that you want to do it.

FROM ME TO YOU . . .

I've been with my partner for a few months and I'm very in love. I want to suggest a threesome between us and my best friend. Am I crazy?
A. F., 18

Not at all. A threesome is just another type of sex. Just because you'd like another person to join you and your partner, doesn't mean to say you don't love them, just that the situation turns you on. You should talk with the people involved, and if they're up for it, go ahead. Whatever you do, bear in mind that this could affect your friendship or relationship. **CHUSITA**

A technique for every taste

MASSAGES: Starting out with your partner by massaging their body, with oils, creams and a lot of tenderness, can give you both plenty of pleasure. It also improves your connection with each other, and keeps you wanting more and more.

BLINDFOLDED: You can cover your partner's eyes, or be blindfolded yourself. Then one of you is in the hands of the other, who can decide how best to enjoy their partner's body—while the other one submits to being surprised.

WITH ICE: Playing with an ice cube is more than just refreshing! You can hold it in your hands and run it over the most sensitive parts of your partner's body. The touch on your hot body will give you goose bumps on your skin, nipples, and pubic hair, awakening surprising new sensations . . .

EROTIC FLAVORS: Certain foods and drinks can really enhance sexual activities! Using pieces of strawberry, whipped cream, or chocolate sauce, you can paint your bodies and then lick them clean!

ROLE-PLAY: Stop being yourself for a little while and become another person for your partner. It can be very erotic! Play-act being doctor and patient, teacher and student, strangers, a firefighter rescuing a helpless victim, or a sexy thief who catches their victim by surprise . . .

IN THE MIRROR: It can be highly arousing to sit in front of a mirror, which allows you to watch your bodies as they move! It helps you experience sex more profoundly, while also feeling like you're watching a film where the two of you are the main characters. Don't be shy!

⚠ **BE SAFE. HAVE FUN.**

GLOSSARY

A

Amazon
Sexual position where the girl is on top of the boy.

anus
Orifice located behind the genitals of both men and women.

C

climax
The highest point of pleasure and arousal. It normally involves an orgasm, although it doesn't have to.

clitoris
Organ located in the female genitals, which pokes out between the outer labia.

coitus
When two people's genitals make direct contact, or when one is inserted into the other.

condom
A rubber sheath, proven to be the best form of protection against STIs and unwanted pregnancies.

cunnilingus
Type of oral sex that involves stimulating the vagina with the mouth.

D

dildo
Sex toy shaped like an erect penis.

E

ejaculation
Expulsion of fluid from the penis, or sometimes the vagina, which usually happens during an orgasm.

erection
The aroused state of the penis when it hardens and rises.

F

fellatio
Type of oral sex that involves stimulating the penis with the mouth.

foreskin
Skin that covers the glans and is attached to it by the frenulum. It is sometimes removed by circumcision.

French kiss

Kiss with tongues.

glans

The head of the penis, which is pink and thick. It's covered by the foreskin.

G-spot

Highly sensitive pleasure point located somewhere inside the vagina.

heavy petting

Activity for couples that is similar to sex, without intercourse itself.

hymen

Membrane that covers part of the vaginal passage, and which generally breaks during penetration.

Kama Sutra

Thousand-year-old Hindi book that lists every imaginable sexual position—not where you should start.

lubricant

A liquid or gel substance that can be applied to add moisture in the vagina or anus, which is necessary for penetration, or to lubricate the penis to reduce friction.

M

masturbation

Genital stimulation, using the hands or by rubbing against something.

missionary

Sexual position where the boy is on top of the girl.

O

orgasm
Release of tension in the body, as a response to sexual arousal. It can involve ejaculation.

P

penis
Long part of the male sex organ.

perineum
Area between the anus and the genitals.

pleasure point
Part of the body that produces arousal when stimulated.

premature ejaculation
When ejaculation is not controlled and it happens too soon.

prostate
Also known as the "P spot." A highly sensitive pleasure point located in the male perineum and anus.

pubis
Triangle-shaped area covered with hair, on the outer part of the genitals. The female pubis is also called the *mons veneris*.

R

rimming
Sexual activity that involves stimulating the anus with the mouth.

S

scissoring
Position in girl-on-girl intercourse, in which the genitals come into contact.

scrotum
Sac that encases the testicles in the male genitals.

semen
Thick liquid that is released by the penis during ejaculation. It contains sperm, which is produced in the testicles.

sexting
Sending erotic images or words via social media. It can lead to sextortion.

sextortion

A type of extortion that involves blackmailing someone with erotic photos.

STIs

Acronym for sexually transmitted infections. They can usually be prevented by using a condom.

T

testicles

Male glands within the body, located in the scrotum, that produce sperm.

testosterone

Hormone produced by the genitals and which drives male sexuality.

V

vagina

Orifice in the female genitals that can be penetrated sexually.

vulva

Outer part of the female genitals, made up of the pubis, the clitoris, and the labia, which encase the vagina.